LOCALIZING THE INTERNET

Anthropology Of Media
Series Editors: John Postill and Mark Peterson

The ubiquity of media across the globe has led to an explosion of interest in the ways people around the world use media as part of their everyday lives. This series addresses the need for works that describe and theorize multiple, emerging, and sometimes interconnected, media practices in the contemporary world. Interdisciplinary and inclusive, this series offers a forum for ethnographic methodologies, descriptions of non-Western media practices, explorations of transnational connectivity, and studies that link culture and practices across fields of media production and consumption.

Localizing the Internet

An Anthropological Account

John Postill

Berghahn Books
New York • Oxford

For Grace

Published in 2011 by

Berghahn Books

www.berghahnbooks.com

Library of Congress Cataloging-in-Publication Data
Postill, John, 1965- Localizing the Internet : an anthropological account /
John Postill.   p. cm. – (Anthropology of the media ; v. 5) Includes
bibliographical references and index. ISBN 978-0-85745-197-2 (alk. paper)
– ISBN 978-0-85745-198-9 (e-book) 1. Internet–Social aspects–Malaysia–
Subang Jaya (Selangor) I. Title. HN655.2.I56.P67 2011 303.48'33095951–
dc23   2011018400

British Library Cataloguing in Publication Data
A catalogue record for this book is available from the British Library.

Printed in the United States on acid-free paper.

ISBN: 978-0-85745-197-2 (hardcopy)
E-ISBN: 978-0-85745-198-9

Contents

List of Figures

Acknowledgements

I wish to thank Marion Berghahn, Ann Przyzycki, Mark Stanton and the rest of the team at Berghahn Books for all their support throughout the making of this book.

The field research was undertaken while I was a research fellow at the University of Bremen (2002 to 2005). I was a member of 'Netcultures', a research group funded by the Volkswagen Foundation, to which I am immensely grateful for its generous financial support. Many thanks are also due to my current research institution, C3RI at Sheffield Hallam University, for their writing-up funding as well as to the Anthropology Department, Vienna University, for a Visiting Professorship that allowed me to further the writing at a critical time.

I am also greatly indebted to Dorle Drackle and the rest of the Netcultures research group – Lenie Brouwer, Sarah Green, Penny Harvey, Oliver Hinkelbein, Monika Rulfs, Paul Strauss, Peter Wade and Tom Wormald – for the superb collective effort and all the good times in Bremen, Amsterdam and Manchester. I thank Richard Diedrich for his early input and regret that he could not continue with us.

I have benefitted enormously from the two Canadian meetings and email exchanges with the sociality group led by Vered Amit whose 'trouble with community' has exerted a decisive influence on my thinking about matters of Internet localization and residential sociality, as will be apparent below. The EASA Media Anthropology Network and the Association of Internet Researchers (AoIR) have been a constant source of information and enlightenment.

In Malaysia, I thank the Economic Planning Unit for granting me a permit to conduct research at very short notice. At my host institution of Universiti Kebangsaan Malaysia (UKM), Professor Shamsul AB was a wonderful host as I prepared for fieldwork in Subang Jaya and Professor

Wan Zawawi chaired one of the most unusual and fruitful seminars I have ever attended, a seminar in which 'the field' came to the university (see Chapter 1).

My Subang Jaya mentor PC Yeoh deserves special mention for all his logistical help, local knowledge and ability to recall ancient jokes. I also wish to thank all the other people in Malaysia who took time out of their busy schedules to help me with my field research, namely Sean Ang, Arpah Bt. Abdul Razak, Azli Niswan, Fausto Barlocco, Robert Chan, Premesh Chandran, KW Chang, Datuk Ahmad Fuad, Goh Ban Lee, Terence Gomez, Jalaluddin, Khai Jin, KJ John, EL Ho, Julian Hopkins, Douglas Ladner, Dato' Lee Hwa Beng, Michelle Lee Guy, Loh Yoke Kean and family, Loo Chin Oon, Lye Tuck-Po, Mahadi Mahussein, Citizen Nades, Agnes Ng, Christopher 'Orchi' Ng, James and Shelley Ongkili, Jeff Ooi, Concerned Subang Jaya Resident, Aftar Singh, Joe Singh, Sim Kwang Yang, Patrick Tan, Raymond Tan, Estnerie s/o Thamotaran, Theresa Ratnam Thong, KY Wong, Timothy Wong and family, Yap Yun Fatt, and Yeoh Seng Guan – with apologies for any omissions!

Earlier versions of most chapters were presented at seminars and conferences held at the universities of Manchester, Kebangsaan Malaysia, Loughborough, Keele, Oxford, Bristol, Swansea, Concordia, Durham, East London, Toronto, Rotterdam, Martin Lüther, Passau, Bilbao, Sheffield Hallam and Vienna, as well as on Steven Clift's DoWire.org site and on my own blog, media/anthropology. I wish to thank all participants at these meetings and blog posters for their questions and comments, as well as two anonymous readers of the manuscript who helped me rethink its organisation and conclusion, suggesting some intriguing connections to legal and political anthropology that I intend to pursue in future work.

I am especially grateful to my partner, Sarah Pink, not only for accompanying me to the field for a period of time, but also for all her encouragement over the long process of writing this book.

Some contents in Chapter 2 are taken from Postill, J. (2010) 'Researching the Internet', *Journal of the Royal Anthropological Institute* (N.S.) 16, 646–50. Parts of Chapters 2 and 7 were originally published as Postill, J. (2008) 'Localizing the Internet Beyond Communities and Networks' in *New Media and Society* 10 (3), 413–31, and parts of Chapter 4 originate in Postill, J. (2010) 'Running Cyburbia: New Media and Local Governance in Subang Jaya' in Yeoh Seng Guan (ed.) *Media, Culture and Power in Malaysia*, Kuala Lumpur: Routledge. These materials are reprinted below with the kind permission of Wiley-Blackwell, Sage and Routledge respectively.

John Postill, Barcelona, 24 January 2011

Preface

In 2002 I took up a Volkswagen Foundation fellowship at Bremen University and joined a team of European anthropologists in a comparative study of local governance and Internet technologies in multiethnic areas of six different countries. Having chosen as my main field site Subang Jaya, a suburb of Kuala Lumpur justly famous in Malaysian technology circles as an Internet 'laboratory', I conducted fieldwork there from 2003 to 2004 followed by additional online research from Britain. I was not disappointed, for in Subang Jaya I found a plethora of Internet projects, ranging from a multimedia library and a 'cybermosque' to several web forums and a 'smart community' initiative. Although the fieldwork went well, on returning home my early attempts at placing these various initiatives along a community-network continuum (with community-like initiatives at one end and network-like initiatives at the other) soon foundered. Eventually I realised that I had fallen into the community/network trap which lies at the heart of Internet Studies and that I seek to avoid in this book. The trap consists of reducing the plurality and flux of social formations that one invariably finds in urban and suburban areas (e.g., peer groups, cohorts, associations, gangs, clans, sects, mosques, factions, families, action committees, mailing lists, online forums, Twitter trends) to a crude community vs. network scheme. This is the misguided idea that our 'local communities' are being impacted upon by a global Network Society and by that 'network of networks' known as the Internet (see Chapter 1).

In search of a way out of this impasse, I dusted off my old undergraduate books and rediscovered the early work of Victor Turner, A.L. Epstein and other members of the Manchester School of Anthropology. I also found unexpected connections between this ancestral body of work and more recent anthropological explorations (e.g., Amit and Rapport 2002,

Gledhill 2000) as well as signs of a renewed interest in their pioneering studies (Evens and Handelman 2006). The Manchester scholars conducted fieldwork in a very different part of the world (British Central Africa) and under radically different historical conditions: the end of Empire. Yet the conceptual issues they confronted were strikingly similar to those I was struggling with after returning from fieldwork in post-colonial Malaysia. The problem boils down to how to study a locality under conditions of rapid social and political change when 'tribal', linguistic and other 'community' groupings appear to be in flux and new kinds of affiliations and social formations are being constantly made and remade, e.g., around novel occupational or recreational practices. Faced with such fluid actualities on the ground, the Manchester scholars moved away from the then predominant structural-functionalist paradigm and towards historical-processual accounts informed by new concepts such as 'field', 'network', 'social drama' and 'arena'.

In *Localizing the Internet* I synthesise this approach with the equally historical and processual field-theoretical model developed by Pierre Bourdieu, best demonstrated in his monograph *The Rules of Art*. Rather than positing the existence of a 'local community' being impacted upon by global networks, my focus is on how variously positioned field agents and agencies in Subang Jaya (residents, politicians, committees, councillors, journalists and others) compete and cooperate over matters concerning the local residents, often by means of the Internet. I call this dynamic set of projects, practices, technologies, and relations 'the field of residential affairs', and what follows is an anthropological account of its uneven development from 1999 to 2009.

The book opens with a photographic essay that introduces some of the key agents in Subang Jaya's field of residential affairs. This is followed by a chronology of the main events, agents and Internet initiatives that have shaped the field from 1992 to the present day. Chapter 1 sets the theoretical and empirical scene by means of an ethnographic vignette that captures some of the main field struggles at a particular point in time. This allows me to define the field of residential affairs as a specific kind of 'Internet field'. Chapter 2 is a critical review of the interdisciplinary and anthropological literature pertinent to the study of Internet localization. Chapter 3 discusses the regional context of the study and the main research methods adopted. Chapter 4 recounts the history of Subang Jaya's field of residential affairs within Malaysia's political-technological environment and reviews those initiatives and groups that lie beyond the field. Chapters 5 to 7 extend the field analysis further through case studies of the personal media practices of leading field practitioners, of two field conflicts (or 'Internet dramas') that broke out in 2004, and of three types of field sociality that have emerged over time. The book ends with a brief recapitulation of the main argument and with a traditional web genre: a list of frequently asked questions (FAQs).

Photo-Essay

Figure 0.1. PC Yeoh (right), a leading Subang Jaya resident and my fieldwork mentor.

My Subang Jaya fieldwork started on 3 May 2003 and concluded on 22 August 2004, although I took a number of breaks during that period to spend some time with my family in Britain. From October 2003 to January of the following year I was accompanied by my partner, the anthropologist Sarah Pink, and by our only child at the time, Vandon, who was 14 months old when he arrived in Malaysia. Our home was a ninth-floor condominium flat in the Subang Jaya precinct of USJ 6.

On 6 December 2003 we attended a fundraising dinner organised by the USJ Residents' Association (USJRA), founded in 1992. Sarah, Vandon and I arrived there with the association's secretary, PC Yeoh, who kindly collected us from the condo as we did not have a car. PC was not only an inveterate teller of classic jokes and an Internet activist, he was also a font of local knowledge and my Subang Jaya research mentor. The dinner was held at a halal restaurant in USJ's business centre. Sarah and I followed Vandon as he wandered off towards the nearby mosque, Al Falaq – known in technological circles as 'the cybermosque' after a municipal project by that name. Sarah took some pictures of the mosque while I helped Vandon up some steep metal steps. When we got back to the restaurant I paid PC Yeoh 50 ringgit (14 US dollars) for the two of us and we joined a group of diners, including some of the earliest settlers in the suburb who arrived in the 1970s. They told me that in those days nobody wanted to come and live out here in the *hutan* (Malay for 'jungle') so the developers decided to entice prospective buyers with semi-furnished houses at very competitive prices.

Figure 0.2. Chatting with the founder of the Subang Jaya e-Community Portal, political blogger and since March 2008 Member of Parliament, Jeff Ooi (right).

We went inside the restaurant and found a table. I was pleasantly surprised to see the busy founder of the Subang Jaya e-Community Portal and political blogger Jeff Ooi; a key figure in the local Internet scene and the first person that I interviewed on arriving in the suburb in May, along with his portal co-administrator, KW Chang (Chapter 3). Jeff told me that a government planning unit together with the municipal council had test-bedded electronic public services in Subang Jaya to the tune of 1.2 million ringgit

(340,000 US dollars). The project had no less than 76 components. Jeff and his fellow activists used to display hyperlinks to the project on their site but had since removed them. I made a mental note to double-check with Chang whether he had kept any of the links. One of the components was called *e-aduan* (e-complaints), Jeff told me, but he could not recall any of the other names. The problem for the council was that the grassroots response had been more encouraging in the rural areas than here in Internet-savvy suburbia. For their part, Jeff and his fellow volunteers had all but discarded the National IT Agenda (NITA), which Jeff regarded as little more than 'bullet points' (see Chapter 4). Instead of 76 components Jeff was happy to pursue only two goals, namely to keep the portal (a) free from political meddling and (b) financially independent from the government.

Figure 0.3. The local resident Premesh Chandran, co-founder and Chief Executive Officer of Malaysiakini.com, the country's most influential independent news media organisation.

Another surprise encounter was with the local resident Premesh Chandran, a friend of Jeff Ooi and the co-founder and CEO of Malaysiakini.com, the most important online newspaper in the country. I did not have the chance to talk to Prem that evening but I had been round to his place in October, just after his thirty-fourth birthday. On that occasion we had talked about my local research and he suggested I interview the ex-chairman of the USJRA, a retired army officer who was now a member of the residents' committee (JKP) set up by the municipal council. We also talked about academic research in Malaysia and about recent changes in Malaysian family life, particularly how in many families today both parents work and the old networks of housewives are no longer there.

The subject somehow moved back to my Internet research. Prem told me that he once sent in a proposal to the National IT Council (NITC) as part of their SJ2005 programme which had aimed at transforming Subang Jaya into a 'smart community' by the year 2005. He wanted to promote 'technopreneurship' among teenagers in Subang Jaya and attended an early meeting. It was soon clear to him, however, that it had all been designed to allocate town council positions to the various political parties that make up Malaysia's ruling coalition (BN), which are appointments made by the Selangor Chief Minister (Menteri Besar): 'It was apparent to me that SJ2005 did not have sufficient political commitment by the local actors to make the project work, especially in terms of the objective of opening up SJ to public participation via the project'.[1] For this reason he did not pursue the matter further.

Figure 0.4. The local Internet activist, online forum participant and peacemaker, Patrick Tan.

Although I did not get a chance to speak to Prem Chandran during the dinner, I did manage to talk to Patrick Tan, a leading resident and co-founder of the Subang Jaya e-Community Portal. Patrick is a natural peacemaker who more than once has had to mediate among warring factions within the locality. Our conversation was difficult at times for I was simultaneously trying to look after Vandon who was being very active that evening. Patrick told me that the chocolate cake I was about to savour was baked locally by appointment to the Sultan of Selangor. The cake was indeed delicious. I then told Patrick that I would have to interview him soon about his role in the founding of the portal which had become such a thriving online meeting place for local residents. With characteristic modesty, he said that he had not really done much and that I could get all the necessary information from Jeff. 'But I need all perspectives!', I protested, to which he smiled in agreement. Still on the subject of the portal, Patrick told me that before he retired he used to suffer from stress-related insomnia: 'People were surprised to find me online at 3 AM but that's because I couldn't go to sleep'.

Figure 0.5. The state assemblyman for Subang Jaya, Dato' Lee Hwa Beng, addressing the local residents.

The guest of honour that evening was a popular local politician with the Chinese component party (MCA) of the ruling coalition, Subang Jaya's state assemblyman, Dato' Lee Hwa Beng. I chatted briefly to Lee before his after-dinner speech. He had tried to contact me to arrange our agree our agreed 'day in the life' session but my mobile phone was down. He invited me to join him the next day on a Walk for Peace scheduled to start from the nearby Monash University campus and I gladly accepted.

Lee is what Everett Rogers (1995) would call an 'early adopter' of technological innovations. In October 1995, when the World Wide Web was still a novelty even in the global North, he launched his own personal website so as to 'further enhance my service to the community', noting on the site that this was 'a revolutionary step' to take for a state assemblyman. Throughout his thirteen-year tenure (1995 to 2008) Lee used his website both to publicise his achievements and to interact with constituents and others, even allowing for dissenting voices. His political strategy was based on what I call 'the *turun padang* imperative' (see Chapter 1). *Turun padang* is a commonly used Malay term that translates as 'to go down to the ground'. In order to gain the trust and support of local residents, powerful figures such as Lee have no choice but to go down to the ground on a regular basis. Only then, or so the political belief goes, will they be in a position to understand and resolve local issues.

Lee started his speech by joking that he was happy to be there even though many of the attendants may not even be his voters. He said it was good to see so many friends from all the different races: Chinese, Indians, Sikhs, Malays, even some foreigners like John from Britain and, addressing a white Australian who had recently arrived in Subang Jaya '…erm, you, sorry but I don't remember your name!' – a remark that caused great merriment. It was good to see this diverse audience, said Lee, because 'sometimes there is racial disharmony; our children have forgotten about harmony and we've had Malays and Chinese fighting, not once but several times'. To tackle this problem, Lee had launched a youth basketball league and other sporting activities. 'People like you are very important', he continued. Then, clearly hinting at the residents' association's inactivity, he added that 'There are some things that the RA has done, not many, but we can do more than dinners'. One of these things was the fight against crime, said Lee, as he entreated the local residents to join his newly created volunteer police force. In effect, he was saying that the proof of the padang is not in the eating but in the doing.

Before leaving for home I caught sight of Joe Singh. Joe is well known in the suburb for his crime prevention activities. He once told me that on one occasion he had a brush with a knife-yielding thug but he wrestled the knife off him. More recently he had caught a flasher who would take pictures of his victims. 'He got a kick out of it', added Joe. On 24 June 2004 the local press reported that Joe had helped to catch a youngster after an attempted theft. The victim's cries for help alerted the neighbours, including Joe:

Figure 0.6. Joe Singh, a local hero and former police volunteer.

One resident, Joe Mahinder Singh, 47, was in his car when the incident happened. 'My instinct told me they would exit to the main road, and I drove over there. My instinct was right,' said the businessman who recently received a letter of commendation from Petaling Jaya police chief Datuk Sheikh Mustafa Sheikh Ahmad in recognition of his efforts in combating crime in the neighbourhood. As he drove to the exit, he rammed into the motorcycle causing the suspects to fall off. They then got up and ran. Joe shouted out at two young boys across the road to stop the thieves, and they managed to grab one. The other managed to escape. A police report has been lodged.[2]

Notes

1. Personal communication from Premesh Chandran, 28 January 2011.
2. http://epaper.thestar.com.my/Daily/skins/sta/navigator.asp?AW=1088050910224.

Chronology

The following is a chronology of the main events, actors and technologies that have shaped Subang Jaya's field of residential affairs from 1992 to 2009. The seven main individual and collective actors are numbered in square brackets. Their trajectories can be visualised in different colours, as entwined historical threads, each adding to the multicoloured fabric of the field of residential affairs.

[1] USJ Residents' Association (USJRA)
[2] State assemblyperson
[3] Subang Jaya municipal council (MPSJ)
[4] Subang Jaya 2005 (SJ2005)
[5] USJ Neighbourhood Watch (nwatch.com.my)
[6] Subang Jaya e-Community Portal (USJ.com.my)
[7] Campaign for the return of local elections to Malaysia

1992 USJ Residents' Association (USJRA) founded by Tony Xavier and other residents [1].

1995 Dato' Lee Hwa Beng (MCA) elected state assemblyman for Subang Jaya, then under the jurisdiction of Petaling Jaya. Launches pesonal website [2].

1997 Subang Jaya municipal council (MPSJ) gazetted by the Selangor State Government [3].

1998 MPSJ officially inaugurated with Datuk Ahmad Fuad as its first municipal president [3].

1999 Birth of SJ2005, the brainchild of corporatised government ICT agency MIMOS. Aimed to make Subang Jaya into a hi-tech 'smart community' by 2005 [4].

1999 Neighbourhood Watch group launched by Raymond Tan in USJ

18 after a spate of robberies [5].

1999   Residents' campaign against a steep rise in local taxes leads to the creation on 26 October of the Subang Jaya e-Community Portal (USJ.com.my), owned by Jeff Ooi [6].

1999   Lee Hwa Beng re-elected as state assemblyman for a second term, 29 November [2].

2000   First steering committee of SJ2005 held in April [4].

2000   In November, Subang Jaya e-Community Portal voted best e-Community project in Malaysia by PIKOM-Computimes and @ MY 2000 [6].

2001   MPSJ creates residents' committees (JKP) system in line with UN Local Agenda 21. Aimed to enhance cooperation between the council and local residents. Officially launched on 10 February by the chief minister of Selangor [3].

2001   Neighbourhood Watch awarded a one-year ICT grant of 1.124 million ringgit (c. 300,000 US dollars) under SJ2005 in August. Other local players feel sidelined, especially MPSJ and USJ.com.my [3] [4] [5] [6].

2002   Residents' committees (JKP) Portal launched by the municipal council in May [3].

2002   Subang Jaya's municipal president, Datuk Ahmad Fuad, wins IT Personality of the Year award [3].

2003   Jeff Ooi takes up blogging on national issues in January. He soon becomes one of Malaysia's leading political bloggers but has less time for local cyberactivism [6].

2003   Fuad steps down as council president to take up a high-profile post in Penang from 1 August. Succeeded by the less dynamic Haji Ad Hakim Borhan [3].

2003   Local Elections Forum held in Subang Jaya, 14 September. Subsequent mailing list remains dormant and initiative makes no impact on the local field of residential affairs [7].

2004   Lee Hwa Beng re-elected as state assemblyman for a third term [2].

2004   On 12 June, a group of residents bearing the USJ.com.my domain name on a banner to protest MPSJ inaction over a blocked drain incur the wrath of Jeff Ooi. A short-lived Internet drama ensues [3] [6].

2004   Residents' Internet, SMS and mass media campaign against the council-approved building of a food court on land earmarked for a police station ends in victory for the residents on 4 October [1] [5] [6].

2004   Asian tsunami appeal launched on 28 December by a group of

Internet activists and endorsed by local politicians. A total of 25, 000 ringgits (c. 7,000 US dollars) donated to the Red Crescent[5] [6].

2005 New SMS Crime Alert System launched at Subang Parade on 25 August [2] [5].

2008 Political upheaval as the young opposition candidate with DAP, Hannah Yeoh, 28, is elected as new state assemblyperson for Subang Jaya in March.

Jeff Ooi, also with DAP, wins a parliamentary seat in Penang. Lee Hwa Beng contests a parliamentary seat but loses and retires from politics [2] [6].

2008 Controversy surrounds USJ.com.my as its forum administrator, KW Chang, removes political threads from the main forum following the opposition's electoral gains in Subang Jaya and other parts of Malaysia [6].

2008 One-fifth of MPSJ councillors now drawn from civil society; no longer 100 per cent political appointees [3].

2009 Police station finally completed on 24 March, after a five-year wait [1] [5] [6].

2009 Debate on whether local council elections should be restored in Malaysia chaired by the state assemblywoman, Hannah Yeoh, 7 June [7].

CHAPTER 1

An Internet Field

On the last day of February 2004, I drove with a group of Subang Jaya residents to Universiti Kebangsaan Malaysia (UKM), on the outskirts of Kuala Lumpur, to present my preliminary findings at a research seminar. I was then halfway through fieldwork and this was a unique opportunity to discuss with key actors some of the questions I was struggling with at the time. It was also a chance, or so I hoped, to 'give something back' to the people who were kindly helping with my research.

On entering the seminar room I realised that virtually the entire spectrum of grassroots Internet projects in Subang Jaya was represented in the audience. This included personnel from the National IT Council (NITC), the corporatised agency MIMOS and the Subang Jaya municipal council as well some of the suburb's leading Internet activists. In addition there were a number of students and scholars for good measure. This mixed audience collapsed two worlds that I had hitherto managed to maintain apart, the worlds of academia and fieldwork. In effect, I had brought the field into the university.

I began by explaining that my research question was 'How does the Internet affect the running (i.e., governance) of multiethnic areas?', and that this was a comparative study with fellow anthropologists working in Britain, the Netherlands and Germany. After reviewing some of the main Internet-related initiatives that I had encountered in Subang Jaya, I argued that the suburb's vocal Internet activism had forced the municipal council to engage with the residents in innovative ways, e.g., by creating residents' committees (JKP) and improving their public services both online and offline. However, the Internet had had no discernible effect on the ethno-sectoral divides that run deep through Malaysian society (see Chapter 3). I also discussed SJ2005, an ambitious federal initiative aimed at transforming Subang Jaya into a hi-tech 'smart community' by the year

2005. I reported that sadly two key SJ2005 partners – the municipal council and MIMOS – had recently parted ways, perhaps over questions of ownership or finance, or for other reasons that I had yet to establish. My tentative conclusion was that SJ2005 was doomed, a prognosis that would prove to be correct (Chapter 4).

The subsequent discussion, very ably chaired by the folk musician and anthropologist Wan Zawawi,[1] was long and eventful. Tempers simmered at times but this being Malaysia they did not boil over. A summary of what was said, and who said it, will serve as an introduction to the complex issues surrounding attempts at transforming Subang Jaya into a 'smart community', discussed in more detail later in the book. It will also give us an entry point into Subang Jaya's field of residential affairs and its Internet dimensions.

One of the first reactions to my talk came from Mohamed Azli Niswan, a 28-year-old municipal council employee with a private sector background in public relations. Azli was at the time in charge of e-Community initiatives in Subang Jaya. He told us that in order to make a difference 'you need time and funding'. When the council was set up in 1997 they were understaffed and few of the staff were IT-literate, so they had to train them first before they could engage with the residents. Having done that, the council were now making steady progress, for instance through four web portals and two hypermedia libraries built for the residents. Azli concluded by rhetorically asking the scholars and federal experts present how well they knew the local council and its 'core business'.

The chair, Wan Zawawi, asked Azli if he could provide an example of a decision taken by the council based on their online engagements with local residents. Azli replied that he regularly 'surfed' the independent residents' portal, USJ.com.my, and that they had followed some of the better suggestions received over email. Moreover, they took their own residents' committees (JKP) very seriously – 'everything coming from JKP is a priority for us' – and the JKP portal was about to be linked to other community portals.

Responding to this intervention, the founder of USJ.com.my and vocal activist Jeff Ooi, introduced himself as 'a resident and a ratepayer' and said that they were not 'bashing' the council on the site. 'We purposively provoke, but we want to listen'. Describing Subang Jaya as a laboratory, he said he was exploiting the potential of the Internet and that this was 'a very exciting journey'. By providing an open channel for discussion, everybody could win. For example, two weeks earlier the council had been 'very responsive' after concerns were raised over a planned dog licence on his community portal as well as on the online newspaper *Malaysiakini*. As a result, the council saw the light and abandoned the ill-conceived scheme. Jeff concluded by saying that the Subang Jaya grassroots was breaking up the old power paradigm whereby the government made all the decisions.

Then Kang Wai Chin from the National IT Council secretariat offered 'a clarification'. She explained that SJ2005 was derived from the National IT Agenda (NITA) headed by the prime minister. As Malaysia moves towards becoming an Information Society the government has realised the importance of building a platform for people to participate in decision-making. So the concept of e-Governance was debated and Subang Jaya was chosen as a laboratory, hence SJ2005. 'Ours is let people decide, not the old paradigm … so we have an InfoSoc conference annually, for the *rakyat* [people] to provide input.'

The social anthropologist Wan Zawawi then asked, tongue-in-cheek, what had become of Malaysia's 'old patronage system' (see Gomez and Jomo 1997) in this brave new world of e-Governance. He also suggested the need to deconstruct the notion of 'community' and to interrogate on what basis certain people come to represent 'the community'. 'And what about those people excluded from the e-community?' he asked. 'Who are they?'

Jeff Ooi then returned to Kang's account, saying that the NITC model was indeed very much part of the old paradigm of government – a transmitter-receiver model in which 'the high-brows at NITC' transmit their great wisdom to passive recipients. He also dismissed the National IT Agenda as little more than 'bullet points'. To this, Kang responded that in 1999 the Internet was still very new. The government were and still are 'passionate about sharing power'. SJ2005 was designed to improve people's lives through a trisectoral partnership between the public sector, the private sector, and the people.

At this point the SJ2005 project manager, Agnes Ng from MIMOS, took the floor. She said that she had been praying for someone like me to conduct such a study. SJ2005 was a concept that she developed by following the existing guidelines, and Jeff Ooi's sweeping statement about NITA being no more than bullet points was baseless. In fact, she added, 'to share with you, NITA is about the whole country being knowledge-based. It's not only about hardware and software; that is the old paradigm …We want e-participation for community-building, a smart community.' She ended by inviting everyone in the room to support their efforts.

Later in the session, the Subang Jaya municipal council (MPSJ) representative, Azli, took up a question I had posed earlier about MIMOS's reported attempts to map the township without having first secured access to the council's database. Azli suggested that it was better to work together. 'If we start up together, we stay together. That's better', adding that 'MPSJ *bukan hanya* [is not only an] implementer' of federal visions. To this, Agnes Ng replied that they had sought permission to access the council's database but were told it was confidential.

The session ended with another MIMOS employee, Sean Ang, arguing that there was no real basis for using the term 'e-Governance' in this context, given that local elections are no longer held in Malaysia.

****

This unusual seminar shows, with rare clarity, some of the main actors' positions within what in this book I am calling Subang Jaya's 'field of residential affairs' – that domain of social practice in which variously positioned human agents and agencies compete and cooperate over matters of concern to local residents, often by means of the Internet. The field of residential affairs is an 'Internet field' in that the set of social relations and practices that sustain it are inextricably entangled with Internet technologies such as email, mailing lists, web portals, online forums, blogs and others. Not only that, the notion of 'the Internet' itself acts as a symbolically charged reference point for field agents as they struggle to articulate a coherent vision of a better future for Malaysia and Subang Jaya on heavily contested discursive terrain. The Internet is, after all, both 'a symbolic totality as well as a practical multiplicity' (Miller and Slater 2000: 16).

Although perhaps not as radically as Chris Kelty's (2008) Free Software programmers, these social agents are 'figuring out things' about their social universes partly through technological experimentation (e.g., by interlinking websites across the governmental divide) and partly through discursive means such as this meeting, which in turn shape subsequent socio-technical innovations. Kelty calls the world of Free Software a 'recursive public' – a uniquely C21 public sphere in which 'geeks' constantly rework the very infrastructures that shape their modes of discourse. By analogy we can speak of Subang Jaya's field of residential affairs as being a 'recursive field' in that field practitioners continually remake the very technological means of their discursive engagements, albeit generally digging less deeply down the programming layers than Kelty's geeks.

As several seminar participants pointed out – and on this we were all agreed! – the township of Subang Jaya is an extraordinary Internet laboratory. Despite attempts at drawing up common agendas such as SJ2005, this suburb is the site of a riotous family of Internet projects by different agents and agencies pursuing their own objectives. The seminar exchanges illustrate well that just as there is no homogenous 'Internet' there is no monolithic 'Malaysian government' acting in unison. Rather what we find is variously positioned government agents across a tangle of organisations who, like their fictional counterparts in countless American television serials, often find themselves at odds with other agents when thrown into the same sphere of action.[2]

Theorising the Field

In his 1958 monograph *Politics in an Urban African Community*, the Manchester School anthropologist A.L. Epstein, a student of Max Gluckman, discusses the emergence of a political and administrative system in a mining town located in the Copperbelt region of Northern Rhodesia, in what today is Zambia. This work still has much to offer the student of local governance and social change, and it is surprisingly pertinent to the present Internet study.

Turning away from the then dominant structuralist-functionalist model and towards historical-processual explanations, Epstein set his study against the canvas of the huge processes of migration and urbanisation that were under way in 1950s Africa. Northern Rhodesia was at the time a profoundly divided society, the main chasm running between Europeans and Africans. In turn, both populations were internally divided along lines of class, ethnicity, occupation and gender. Yet at the same time there was a high degree of interdependence across the divides, numerous 'bonds of co-operation' linking together Africans and Europeans within 'a single field of social relations' (1958: xii).

In Copperbelt towns, a relatively stable sociopolitical framework was provided by the mine, the municipal council and the district office (1958: xiv). District commissioners had no say in the running of the mine township, which was a power unto itself (1958: 21). Africans saw commissioners as 'remote Olympian beings who resided in the Government Offices' away from the mines (1958: 22). In the interstices of this framework, though, Epstein found 'a continuous flux in which new groups and associations are constantly springing up' (1958: xiv). Many of these social formations were ephemeral, but they nonetheless left traces on the field of social relations.

The emerging urban system consisted of 'many different sets of social relations or spheres of social interaction' and was riddled with 'ambiguity and inconsistency', not least around contested notions of 'tribalism' (1958: xvii). Epstein stresses the unevenness of social change across what I call 'the field of residential affairs': that field of practice in which local authorities, residents, firms and other social agents compete and cooperate over residential matters. 'The factors making for social change and development operate over the whole of this field, and are present in every sphere; but they do not impinge upon these spheres with the same weight, or at the same time' (Epstein 1958: xvii).

Transplanting these ethnographic observations from a post-war African mining town to an early C21 South East Asian suburb is not as far-fetched as it may seem at first. Although the historical and cultural circumstances are of course vastly different, there are some striking parallels between Epstein's and my own study. Like Epstein, during fieldwork I found myself in the midst of emergent processes of 'production of locality' (Appadurai 1996), finding both the makings of a politico-administrative framework (in my case, centred on the Subang Jaya municipal council, founded in 1997) as well as a more fluid realm in which various residential associations and initiatives were being constantly formed and transformed, many of them as ephemeral as those described by Epstein for the Copperbelt.

Moreover, I found that processes of change were unevenly spread across the field of residential affairs, with some regions of the field changing more rapidly than others. For example, the fight against crime is an ecumenical issue that has brought together people and agencies from across the governmental divide in Subang Jaya. Crime prevention initiatives led by residents have received governmental support, mass media coverage and undergone considerable technological development, including new mobile technologies. By contrast, a campaign to reinstate local elections in Malaysia that sought to mobilise Subang Jaya residents was short-lived and made no impact on the field of residential affairs (see below).

My model of residential politics rests on the proposition that every locale in which humans reside (every village, hamlet, neighbourhood, ward, suburb, borough, mining town, and so on) must by necessity have a field of residential affairs. This term allows us to capture within a single analytical net both state and non-state agents whilst eschewing existing notions which either come with tacit normative assumptions that are best avoided (e.g., local governance, community activism, community development) or are either too broad (local politics) or too narrow (local activism, residential activism) to address this study's central question, namely to what extent the Internet has altered relations between Subang Jaya's local authorities and its residents.

Of course, exactly who the various interested parties are in any given locality, and to what extent they each belong to the broad 'state' vs. 'non-state' agent categories, is a matter for empirical investigation on the ground. For instance, the main parties encountered by Epstein (1958) in the Copperbelt were the colonial district officer, the mine authorities and the workers' representatives. By contrast, in a 1960s Achehnese village in Indonesia, the field action at a specific point in time was dominated by a modernist ulama, his Sufi antagonists, the village headman, and a local police sergeant (Jayawardena 1987, in Gledhill 2000: 132–33). At around the same time, among the Chagga of Mount Kilimanjaro (Tanzania) the key local formation was the 'lineage-neighbourhood complex' which amounted to 'an effective rule-making and sanction-applying social nexus' largely outside the state's legal apparatus (Falk Moore 2000: 72). When Nyerere's socialist state introduced the ten-house cell system with locally elected leaders, this merely added a new strand to relations that were already multiplex. This new system made little difference to the 'permeable but dominant' lineage-neighbourhood complex (2000: 73–74). Finally, in a mid-1980s conflict over a water pump studied by Gledhill in a Mexican village, the main players in the field of residential affairs were the former water supply administrator, the local Catholic priest, his largely female followers, and a 'male faction' alarmed by their women's political assertiveness (Gledhill 2000).

Whatever the local circumstances, we shall have to pay heed both to enduring structural cleavages within the field of residential affairs and to micro-historical contingencies (Gledhill 2000). We will also have to place the field in the context of wider translocal relationships and processes – and in most locales today, within the multi-tiered administrative and political structure of the state (Falk Moore 2006). To use Bourdieuan terminology, this will entail paying close attention to the relative autonomy (or its opposite, heteronomy) of the field of residential affairs from the fields of local government and local party politics. In turn, these fields themselves exist in a dynamic power relationship to other fields, both at the local level (such as local business, local religion) and at higher administrative levels.

In addition to having two or more main sectors, the field of residential affairs exhibits both 'stations' and 'arenas'. Adapting Giddens' (1984: 119) notion of time-geographical 'stations' that social agents traverse and reproduce in the course of their day-to-day activities (homes, nurseries, schools, workplaces, mosques), I will define 'field stations' as those 'stopping places' in which field agents interact with other agents, ideas and technologies on a regular basis, an interaction that in turn (re)produces the station. Examples of such stations would include a leading resident's daily posting of news and/or commentary on a local web forum, an elected politician's weekly surgery with her constituents, or the regular public meetings of a parish council. For a local leader, the regular presence in such settings is an essential part of the work of maintaining good working relations with allies and supporters. By the same token, a prolonged absence from such stations is likely to undermine a leader's position within the field of residential affairs, a field suffused with metaphors of co-presence, collaboration and rootedness. Remarks such as 'The mayor is aloof, he never comes down to the ground' or 'And she calls herself a community leader? When was the last time she mucked in like the rest of us?' do not bode well for a local leader.

So far the picture of the field of residential affairs I have painted is one of Giddensian routinisation and recursivity – the predictable cycles of modern agents as they go about coordinating their activities and (re) producing their practices in real clock-and-calendar time (Postill 2002). But to complete the picture we also need to consider those irregular, often unpredictable patterns of social action that disrupt the regular schedules of a field of practice. The now classic political anthropology of the Manchester scholar Victor Turner (1974) is particularly pertinent here. Borrowing from Turner, I define a 'field arena' as 'a bounded spatial unit in which precise, visible antagonists, individual or corporate, contend with one another for prizes and/or honour' (1974: 132–33). Field arenas are 'explicit frames' in which leading practitioners take major decisions in public view and 'nothing is left merely implied' (1974: 134). Arenas are often stations that have temporarily morphed from being convivial settings to sites of conflict in which individual leaders must state clearly where they stand in an unresolved dispute. It is common for these disputes to centre on a leader's perceived breach of the field's existing moral order, a type of political turmoil known as a 'social drama' that will only be solved after appropriate 'redressive action' has been taken by the offending party (Turner 1974, Eyerman 2008). Private doubts about a leader's ability or commitment to a residential cause may surface onto the public realm in these increasingly digitally mediated arenas, e.g., through SMS texts to the leader demanding that they declare their unambiguous, public support for a given cause via a campaign blog (see Chapter 6 and Arnold et al. 2008).

Subang Jaya's field of residential affairs can be represented in the form of an inverted T or ⊥. The vertical axis represents Malaysia's three-tiered system of government (local, state and federal) whilst the horizontal axis stands for the local level of residential governance, with the voluntary sector to the left of the axis, the municipal council at the intersection and the private sector to the right of the vertical axis. These three local-level sectors (voluntary, public and private) can be regarded as subfields of the total field which have evolved their own characteristic logics and dynamics. Thus, within the voluntary subfield leading residents such as Jeff Ooi will endeavour to assert their autonomy from the governmental subfield (to recall his seminar intervention: 'I am a resident and a ratepayer'). Meanwhile both politicians and councillors will strive to demonstrate their tireless dedication to resolving local issues. Furthermore, each subfield has its own 'fundamental law' (Bourdieu

1993). That of the governmental subfield in Subang Jaya is the law of *tu-run padang* – which as previously mentioned is a Malay phrase meaning 'to go down to the ground' that is frequently invoked to either praise or criticise the behaviour of politicians and councillors. A regular presence 'on the ground' is regarded by residents not as an end in itself but as the necessary precondition for understanding and solving local issues. For its part, the non-governmental subfield abides by the law of selfless volunteerism. To be well regarded by their peers, local residents are expected to freely volunteer their time and labour in exchange for symbolic not financial rewards. No local leader, however charismatic, well-connected or technologically sophisticated, is above the laws of the field of residential affairs. Finally, the commercial subfield abides by the maxim of 'business is business' (Bourdieu 1993). Although many private firms in Subang Jaya such as developers, hypermarkets and shopping malls are only too happy to sponsor 'community' events in exchange for publicity, the unassailable logic of their local activities is profit-making.

Notes

1. See http://voize.my/arts-culture/dr-wan-zawawi-pioneering-malaysian-folk-musician.
2. On the need to disaggregate 'the state' ethnographically, see Krohn-Hansen and Nustad (2005).
3. Contrast this with the four-tiered governance system of European Union states, with the European Commission (EC) at the apex.

CHAPTER 2

Localizing the Internet

Until the mid-1990s the number of Internet users worldwide was small and most users could not help but communicate with others at great distances. But as the number of users and sites continue to grow at an explosive rate, so do the possibilities for connecting and interacting with people, firms and public institutions in our own locality via the Internet. In many respects, the Internet is becoming 'more local' (Davies and Crabtree 2004). The countless processes of Internet localization currently unfolding around the globe pose a set of logistical, methodological and conceptual challenges to researchers. Logistically, they demand of researchers that they spend sufficient time in a local setting in order to get to know – both online and offline – those who live, work and play there; studying these processes 'at a distance' simply will not do. Methodologically, it renders the distinction between online and offline social domains even more problematic than it has been hitherto (Hine 2000), more so as Internet and mobile technologies continue to converge. Conceptually, the challenge is how to keep track of the fast pace of technological change while avoiding the default position whereby a seemingly stationary 'local community' is assumed to be impacted upon by 'global' technologies (see Miller and Slater 2000: 1–25).

Two approaches to the study of Internet localization stand out in the extant literature, both hinging on the notions of community and network.[1] First, there is the 'community informatics' approach in which researchers study a 'local community' and assess its specific technological needs.[2] Researchers of this persuasion regard local communities as 'the bedrock of human development' (Gurstein 2004). Without communities, they argue, humans would be adrift in a dehumanising global (dis) order. To resist the onslaught of capitalism and become empowered, they suggest, local communities must take control of the very networked technologies that threaten their survival (Gurstein et al. 2003).

Second, there is the 'networked individualism' approach led by the social network analyst Barry Wellman. Wellman has denounced the smuggling of obsolete notions of community from an earlier period of North American community studies into Internet localization studies. Where the old communities had 'streets and alleys', internet researchers are now imagining communities bound 'by bits and bytes' (Hampton and Wellman 2003). For Wellman this is an analytical cul-de-sac, for the crucible of North American sociality has long ceased to be the local neighbourhood (Wellman and Leighton 1979). This does not mean, Wellman insists, that communities have disappeared. Rather they have survived in the form of geographically dispersed 'personal communities', i.e., personal networks (cf. Pahl 2005). The Internet merely reinforces a global trend towards networked individualism that was already well under way (Castells 2001, Wellman et al. 2003).[3]

Despite their differences, both approaches to Internet localization share a heavy reliance on the entwined notions of community and network. Although ever popular among Internet scholars, policy-makers and activists, both terms have had troubled careers as anthropological concepts. These conceptual difficulties, I suggest, demand closer attention if we intend to further our understanding of how the Internet is becoming – among other things – 'more local'. Here I shall merely sketch them out, starting with the notion of community.

The Community/Network Paradigm

The anthropologist Vered Amit (2002a) has reviewed 'the trouble with community' as a theoretical concept. Amit argues that the term's strong emotional resonance makes it an ideal choice in public rhetoric, even though its empirical referent is seldom specified, or indeed specifiable. Amit cautions that expressions of community always 'require sceptical investigation rather than providing a ready-made social unit upon which to hang analysis' (2002a: 14). Relying on emotionally charged, bounded notions such as community, diaspora, nation, or ethnic group is unwise, she adds, for there are numerous sets of social relations that cannot be brought under these banners. Such sets include neighbours, co-workers and leisure partners – people who many nevertheless share 'a sense of contextual fellowship' that can be 'partial, ephemeral, specific to and dependent on particular contexts and activities' (Rapport and Amit 2002: 5). Countering the often heard response that community remains a valid term because it is a notion dear to millions of people around the world, Amit urges us not to conflate cultural categories with actual social groups.

This point has strong implications for the study of Internet activism and other forms of social mobilisation, since 'the assignation of membership in a particular cultural category does not tell us, in itself, which categories will actually be drawn on for the mobilisation of social relations' (Amit 2002a: 18). For instance, members of a local organising committee may tell a researcher that all revellers at a street party are one 'community'. It does not follow that the same set of people will mobilise against the building of an airport in their vicinity. In sum, community merits attention as a polymorphous folk notion widely used both online and offline, but it is of little use as an analytical concept with an identifiable empirical referent. As one Internet researcher put it during a discussion on the ontological status of community: 'Fears of goblins do not goblins make'.[4]

One variant of this problematic notion that has gained popularity in recent times is the concept of 'communities of practice' (Wenger 1998). Examples include families, work teams, sports teams, peer groups, virtual worlds and countless other groupings. These formations are said to be ubiquitous and to display three main features. First, community members relate to one another through 'mutual engagement'; second, they all pursue the same goal or endeavour; third, members share a common linguistic, stylistic and practical repertoire that is crucial to their sense of identity as a group (Barton and Tusting 2005: 2).

This is not the place for a critique of this concept, whose virtues and shortcomings have been widely discussed in various literatures. For our present purposes, a brief explanation of why I will not be adopting it in this study will suffice. The first reason is that the phrase 'community of practice' contains within it the emotive, normative ideal of a benign 'community' that I have just questioned. Moreover, as a number of authors have pointed out, there is an implicit assumption of boundedness and homogeneity at work in this notion (Barton and Tusting 2005: 8; Gee 2005). Finally, community of practice proponents have played down questions of power and conflict (2005: 10) that are central to the subject-matter and field-theoretical approach of the present study. This is not to say that there is no value to this concept, but rather that it would not be of much use in the study of the highly dynamic, conflictual domain of life that is contemporary suburban politics. As explained earlier, I have found the coinage 'field of residential affairs' to be far better suited to this task.

Turning now to network, in the 1950s and 1960s this notion appeared to offer anthropologists an exit route from the entrapments of structural-functionalism (Sanjek 1996). By following individuals across social fields they hoped to be able to capture the open-ended nature of much social life, particularly in the urban settings where growing numbers of anthropologists were now finding themselves (Mitchell 1969, Amit 2007). However, they came to an impasse as they pursued ever more systematic 'morphological calculations' within increasingly small units of analysis (Amit 2007). As a consequence, social network analysis (SNA) was all but abandoned by social anthropologists in the 1970s (Sanjek 1996).

Interestingly it was precisely in the 1970s, as computers became more widely available, that SNA became popular with other social scientists (Freeman 2007). One milestone was Granovetter's (1973) 'strength of weak ties' thesis in which he showed that jobseekers in Boston found their 'weak' connections (e.g., with friends of friends) to be more useful in the job market that the 'strong' bonds of close friendship and kinship. This work helped to popularise SNA among North American sociologists and economists (Knox et al. 2006: 118). Today SNA is used in a vast range of research areas, including mental illness, the spread of diseases and information, the sociology of organisations and Internet studies (Freeman 2007).

In recent years we have seen renewed anthropological interest in social networks, but anthropologists are still wary of this concept. Two main approaches can be discerned: (a) those anthropologists who 'found' networks in the field, so to speak (e.g., when working with transnational activists, development workers or technocrats – see Edelman 2005, Green et al. 2005, Juris 2008, Knox et al. 2006, Riles 2000) and (b) those anthropologists who wish to rethink this problematic notion of 'network' even though it is not a key folk notion or organising principle in their own field sites (e.g., Amit 2007, Hinkelbein 2008 and below, Horst and Miller 2006, Moeran 2002).

Green, Harvey and Knox's (2005) *Current Anthropology* article, 'Scales of Place and Networks', belongs to the first category. These authors conducted ethnographic research in the second half of the 1990s and early 2000s among staff in various publicly funded digital projects in Manchester, UK. The main rationale for these projects, as seen by their champions, was to propel Manchester and its environs to the forefront of developments towards a European Network Society. Everywhere they looked, the researchers found an 'imperative to connect', that is, an overriding ambition on the part of ICT policy makers and their allies to use the idea of networks to link European projects, organisations, cities, and regions across divides of geography, language and culture. The aim was not to create virtual spaces (cf. Boellstorff's Second Life below) but rather 'new networks of located connection' (2005: 817).

What was new, argue Green et al., was 'the fantasy of open, flexible, rapid, and implicitly "flattened" connection – connection with no centres, boundaries, hierarchies, or fixity – that would overcome diversity and incompatibility without requiring them to disappear' (2005: 817). Yet this idealised imperative to connect (an imperative that regards disconnection as a problem demanding a solution – see also Hinkelbein 2008) overlooked the constraints, tangles and disconnects that invariably accompany all human endeavour. More specifically, the Castells-inspired idea of fluid, interlocal networks as the dominant social and economic logic of our era – Castells's work was often invoked by informants – concealed the extent to which the digital projects in question were entangled in specific place-making projects around entities such as 'Manchester', 'Europe' or 'Britain'. The problem was not that project champions were technological determinists, conclude the authors. Rather they were driven by the hope and desire that all the various technical, personal and political incompatibilities besetting the projects would be somehow overcome. Alas, they were not.

Vered Amit (2007) belongs to group (b), i.e., those anthropologists who do not study networks as folk metaphors but rather wish to rethink and rehabilitate this anthropological concept. Amit urges us to reclaim the original promise of network as a notion that offers qualitative researchers the freedom to explore interpersonal links without any prior assumptions about what kinds of links or collectives are more worthy of study (Hannerz 1980). She exemplifies this position with a Granovetter-inspired study of expatriate consultants struggling to maintain personal networks across vast geographical expanses. This echoes a review article by Knox et al. (2006) who warn about the lack of critical engagement with key SNA notions such as 'whole network'. While whole populations are admittedly extremely difficult to research, drawing an arbitrary boundary around the network to be investigated in order to overcome this problem (e.g., by limiting the study to children in a few school classes) contradicts the fundamental idea of networks being unbounded and cutting across enduring groupings and organisations.

The present study also belongs to the second category, for the Internet activists and other local agents I met in suburban Kuala Lumpur, although very familiar with the idea of 'networking', were far more interested in 'community building' than in networks. My prime concern, though, is not with the limitations or potentialities of community and network as theoretical concepts, but rather with their unchallenged dominance in the Internet localization literature. This paradigmatic dominance blinkers our view of the actual Internet practices of local authorities, firms and residents around the globe.

The Public Sphere

One available exit from the community/network trap is the Habermasian concept of 'public sphere'. Holub (in Webster 1995: 101–2) defines public sphere as '[a]n arena, independent of government [and market] ... which is dedicated to rational debate and which is both accessible to entry and open to inspection by the citizenry. It is here ... that public opinion is formed'.

Despite Habermas's insistence that the public sphere (*Öffentlichkeit*) was a phase in European history not a universal phenomenon, most new media scholars have used it as a normative, democratic ideal that all modern societies should aspire towards (Benson 2007, Chadwick 2006). Thus, Dahlberg (2001) has evaluated the citizen-led initiative Minnesota e-Democracy, built around an email list forum, against five predefined public sphere criteria: autonomy from state and market, reciprocal critique, reflexivity, sincerity, and discursive inclusion. The problem with Dahlberg's strategy is that it prescribes what counts as a domain worthy of investigation. Like community, public sphere is used both as a 'rhetorical token' (Benson 2007: 3) and as a normative notion that guides research away from what is, and towards what ought to be.

A further difficulty with this concept is that its advocates, starting with Habermas, have failed to explore how public spheres are internally differentiated (Peters 2002: 4; Benson 2007: 4). '[W]hatever its qualities, any public sphere is necessarily *a socially organised field*, with characteristic lines of division, relationships of force, and other constitutive features' (Calhoun 1992: 38, quoted in Benson 2007: 4, my emphasis).

Field Theory

In view of these operational difficulties with the notion of public sphere, I wish to propose instead the concept of 'field' as one possible way of overcoming the community/network impasse.[5] Put simply, a field is an organised domain of practice in which social agents compete and cooperate over the same public rewards and prizes (Martin 2003). One advantage of field is that it is a neutral, technical term lacking the normative idealism of both public sphere and community. Moreover, field theorists have developed a sophisticated vocabulary that is increasingly being recruited to the study of media (Benson 2007, Benson and Neveu 2005, Couldry 2007, Hesmondhalgh 2006, Peterson 2003). More pertinent to the case at hand, field theory offers us a framework with which to analyse the Internet-mediated relations between local authorities and residents by treating these two parties not as discrete entities but rather relationally, as two sectors of a porous, conflict-prone realm that I am calling 'the field of residential affairs'. I define this as a domain of practice in which variously positioned agents and agencies compete and cooperate over matters that concern the residents of a given locality, often by means of the Internet.

Although today we associate field theory with Pierre Bourdieu (1993, 1996), this theory has a far longer history originating in physics and Gestalt psychology (Martin 2003). Bourdieu was critical of social network analysis for what he regarded as its naive commitment to interaction as the basis of human life, and he developed his field theory in opposition to SNA. He argued that by concentrating on people's visible interactions and ties, SNA practitioners fail to grasp the invisible network of objective relations binding human agents within a common cultural space (such as France) and its fields of practice (e.g., art, sociology, photography). For Bourdieu, SNA conflates structure with interaction, exaggerating the importance of 'social capital', i.e., the capital that accrues from social connections, whilst neglecting other species of capital such as cultural and symbolic capital (Knox et al. 2006). For example, two Parisian artists who have never met may nonetheless possess similar amounts of symbolic capital (prestige, renown, status) and occupy neighbouring positions within the field of art. In Bourdieu's field theory, it is agents' relative positions and amounts of field-specific capital that matter, not with whom they interact.

In *Localizing the Internet* I draw on Bourdieu's field lexicon, but I find his dismissal of interaction unhelpful on two accounts. First, it is hard to envisage how one could study the Internet without considering its interactivity, e.g., the ease with which users of mailing lists, blogs and micro-blogs can reply to posts (on media and interaction, see Thompson 1995). Second, Bourdieu's opposition to SNA's interactionism conceals the fact that within the SNA tradition there has always existed a tension between its interactionist (or connectionist) and its structural (or field) strands. Whilst network analysts who adopt a contact approach do indeed map interactions and ties onto 'sociograms' (e.g., de Nooy 2003: 313), field-oriented SNA practitioners are more interested in 'structural relations usually opaque to actors' (Knox et al. 2006: 117).

In fact, a number of scholars have successfully managed to graft the notion of interaction onto their field analyses. Thus, Wouter de Nooy (2003: 323) has shown how the interactions of literary critics and female authors in the 1970s helped to establish and naturalise the category of 'feminist literature' within the Dutch literary field. To this theorist, a field of practice is shaped by objective power relations 'insofar as they influence the interaction within the field' (de Nooy 2003: 323). Similarly, Victor Turner's (1974) reconstruction of a failed uprising in colonial Mexico, the Hidalgo Insurrection, tracks the interactions that took place in a series of 'arenas' over a period of six months. Turner understands the insurrection to have been a 'social drama' unfolding across a rapidly shifting political field made up of the people, institutions and other resources mobilised to assist or thwart the rebellion (cf. Zald and McCarthy 1988).

Suburban Frontiers

As mentioned above, Victor Turner was a leading exponent of the Manchester School of Anthropology whose members were keenly interested in social change, particularly in the urbanising regions of Central and Southern Africa during decolonisation (Evens and Handelman 2006). The situation there was curiously analogous to that faced today by suburbanites in many parts of the world. Like rural migrants in the booming urban areas of post-war Africa (Epstein 1958), many present-day suburbanites find themselves in densely populated settlements with inadequate social and public facilities. The result is the mushrooming of ad hoc initiatives seeking to resolve the more pressing problems.

Newly built suburbs are ideal settings in which to rethink our current dependency on community and network as the paradigmatic notions in the study of Internet localization. These are frontiers where newly arrived people, technologies and ideas shape one another in unforeseeable ways. Over time new forms of residential sociality arise out of this flux, as residents, private firms, local authorities and other human agents strive to 'produce locality' (Appadurai 1996). In such unsettled conditions, any attempt at positing an existing 'local community' being impacted upon by a globalising 'network logic' is bound to fail.

New suburbs are particularly well suited to the study of emerging forms of residential sociality linked to 'banal activism' – an activism focused on seemingly mundane issues such as traffic congestion, waste disposal and petty crime.[6] Banal activism has been neglected by Internet scholars, particularly in East and South East Asia. The two main suburban Internet studies to date to discuss residential sociality and banal activism provide useful entry points but are marred by their adherence to the community/network paradigm (see also Arnold et al. 2008).

The better known study was conducted by Keith Hampton in the Toronto suburb of 'Netville' (a pseudonym) from 1997 to 1999. Hampton combined survey research with participant observation in this new 'wired-up' locality to study the impact of the Internet on 'local community' (Hampton and Wellman 2003). He found that the internet helped Netville's settlers to make new friends and acquaintances both in their own immediate neighbourhoods and across the suburb, as well as being able to maintain older ties with geographically dispersed friends and relatives. Residents with the most online contacts also tended to have the most offline contacts in the suburb. In accordance with Granovetter's 'strength of weak ties' dictum, local residents drew on their new contacts to make further contacts for information, socialising, mutual aid and so on, in the process increasing their local 'social capital'. The web of social ties thus created had important political implications as well, for it allowed residents to mobilise effectively when the developers attempted to withdraw the very technologies that had facilitated the collective production of sociality (Hampton 2003, Hampton and Wellman 2003).

A more recent study was conducted by Yael Levanon in the Tel Aviv suburbs of Ramat Beit-Shemesh and Modiin, the former settled by orthodox Jews, the latter by both religious and secular families. Levanon's starting point was, like Hampton's, the North American literature on the reported decline in community social capital (Putnam 1995, see also Putnam 2000). Her aim was to study 'community networking' and its effect on local ties. On the basis of a questionnaire delivered to users of two local mailing lists, Mesch and Levanon (2003) argue that the Internet has allowed residents to find like-minded others across their suburb with whom to exchange information, socialise and cooperate – a finding that echoes the Netville study. Another similarity was the use of the Internet for banal activism, in the Israeli case to oppose the building of a new mall that would open on Saturdays and offer non-kosher food. Yet, in contrast to their North American counterparts, the Tel Aviv settlers had little need for the Internet at the immediate neighbourhood level, for in Israel the neighbourhood remains a fulcrum of sociality.

These two studies further our understanding of Internet localization in suburban settings in a number of ways. First, they point at cross-cultural similarities as well as contrasts in the Internet-shaped making of suburban socialities. In both countries, suburban families with young children and dual-career parents are driven by the imperative to find and maintain a social environment conducive to family-building and class reproduction (see Miller 1995), an imperative that shapes their use of Internet technologies. However, the specific 'banal' issues that matter to residents can vary greatly from one locale to another, even within the same country. For instance, plans to build a non-kosher restaurant were resisted by orthodox, not secular, Jews in suburban Tel Aviv. Second, the two studies demonstrate the continued usefulness of Granovetter's theory of weak ties in contexts other than Boston's 1970s job market (see also Haythornthwaite 1998, Amit 2007), enabling their authors to correct the overemphasis on 'strong', affective ties found in the community informatics literature (Hampton 2003). Third, these studies shed light on the critical importance of two specific 'Internet affordances' (Wellman et al. 2003), namely its interactivity and asynchronicity, to suburban residents who are able to engage with local issues despite their work and childcare commitments.

There are, however, some shortcomings as well. First, both studies are examples of the connectionist strand of social network analysis discussed earlier. This weakens their explanatory power when it comes to structural or 'field' questions. Murali Venkatesh (2003: 344–45) has broached such field-related questions with reference to Hampton's Netville research and suggested, following Melucci (1996), that collective action is always tethered to relational structures (or fields) that constrain action, although 'breakthrough social agency is always possible'. This relational line of inquiry is not pursued, though, in Hampton's own work.

Both studies are furthermore caught up in the community/network semantic tangle, for instance by making contradictory use of the term 'community'. Thus, in Mesch and Levanon's (2003) analysis, community is used in places to refer to a pre-existing, unspecified collectivity ('the local community'), in others to the future outcome of an ongoing effort ('community-building'), yet in others to the suburb in its entirety ('the extended community') as opposed to the neighbourhood. As I have argued earlier, community is a vague notion favoured in public rhetoric, not a sharp analytical tool with an identifiable empirical object. Amit (2002a: 14) puts it well: 'Invocations of community … do not present analysts with clear-cut groupings so much as signal *fields* of complex processes through which sociality is sought, rejected, argued over, realised, interpreted, exploited or enforced' (my emphasis).

The present account is precisely an anthropological reconstruction of such a 'field of complex processes' and its Internet-related socialities.

Anthropology and the Internet

My approach is framed by the anthropology of media (Postill 2006, Postill 2009), and more specifically by existing anthropological studies of Internet media. The turn of the millennium saw the publication of four important Internet ethnographies: Hakken's (1999) *Cyborgs@Cyberspace*, Zurawski's (2000) *Virtuelle Ethnizität*, Hine's (2000) *Virtual Ethnography*, and Miller and Slater's (2000) *The Internet: An Ethnographic Approach*. The authors of these pioneering studies grappled with difficult questions that still occupy Internet researchers today, such as interaction and identity in cyberspace, the virtual vs. the actual, technological appropriation and obsolescence, the digital divide, or the prospects and limitations of online ethnography.

Of the four monographs, it is arguably Miller and Slater's that best fore-shadows more recent studies, including the present book. These authors investigated the late 1990s uses of the Internet by Trinidadians both at home and abroad. Distancing themselves from the ICT domestication literature (see Silverstone and Hirsch 1994) they argue that Trinidadians are not merely 'appropriating' the Internet; rather they are putting themselves on the global stage via the Internet just as much as users in metropolitan centres. Miller and Slater take issue with much of the earlier Internet literature for its postmodern celebration of fluid/blurred online identities, which they found had little bearing on Trinidadian uses of the Internet, and for its assumption that 'cyberspace' is a placeless 'virtual' domain divorced from actual physical places. Instead they advise Internet scholars to start from the opposite assumption, namely that online domains are part of – not apart from – everyday offline contexts. To these ethnographers, the Internet involves 'many different technologies, practices, contexts: it is no one thing, and our study encompassed a wide range of contexts, from ways of doing business to socializing in cybercafes' (Miller and Slater 2000: 3). One key finding was Trinidadians' seemingly 'natural' affinity with the Internet, even in low-income areas where many people's access was mediated by friends or family. This finding complicated their pre-fieldwork expectations of a vast 'digital divide' separating rich and poor Trinidadians – and indeed Trinidadians from Westerners (2000: 27).

In what follows I review a small number of anthropological studies (Boellstorff 2008, Hinkelbein 2008, Kelty 2008, Roig 2008) completed or published in 2008 following research trajectories that differ notably from those of Miller and Slater. First, they were conducted largely in metropolitan areas of the global North and among mostly white middle-class Internet innovators. Second, rather than being about 'the Internet' in general they each focus on a single Internet platform or field of practice (Second Life, Free Software, Internet filmmaking, digital integration). Third, many of the Internet technologies and practices described in these studies were either not in existence or still in their infancy at the time of Miller and Slater's research. Finally, two of the four texts are in languages other than English (i.e., German and Catalan) – no small matter given the overwhelming dominance of Anglophone scholarship to date.

In spite of these contrasts, Miller and Slater's discussion of the main challenges facing late 1990s Internet ethnographers are still highly pertinent to all four studies, as we shall see shortly. The studies' chief contributions to the field are the strong case made for the existence of virtual places, detailed accounts of a wide range of new and old Internet practices, and the rigorous conceptual work around notions such as 'third place', 'recursive public', 'collaborative filmmaking' and 'digital integration'. Like their precursors, these studies provide further evidence that we are not at the dawn of a new planetary era in which a totalising 'techno-logic' (of networks, information, knowledge craft, or some other kind) will impose itself on all other cultural logics. Instead, together they confirm the ongoing differentiation of the Internet into an expanding universe of 'technologies, practices, contexts' – to use Miller and Slater's apt formulation.

A Virtual Place

Let us start with Tom Boellstorff's *Coming of Age in Second Life*. This is an ethnographic account of the 3D online environment Second Life. The rationale of the project was both methodological and pedagogical (Kelty 2009): Boellstorff wished to explore what ethnography can teach us about 'virtual worlds' such as Second Life (SL). With this aim in mind, from June 2004 to January 2007 he 'took up residence' in SL as the avatar Tom Bukowski. *Coming of Age* describes in fascinating detail the everyday lives and social relations of the SL 'residents' encountered by Bukowski during his stay there. Tackling Miller and Slater's challenge head-on (2008: 62), Boellstorff does not see the need to embed online sociality in the 'actual world', setting out instead to explain 'inworld' practices in their own terms, not as a pale reflection or simulation of offline practices. These inworld practices include weaving, building, trading, chatting, dancing, making love, flying and many others besides.

The most intriguing part of Boellstorff's argument is his extended discussion of SL as a place. Questioning the media studies habit of regarding virtual worlds as the antithesis of place-making, he argues that SL is a 'new kind of place', or more precisely, a 'set of locations' where new forms of human sociality and craft (techne) are flourishing (2008: 91). This is the fortuitous result of two separate 1970s breakthroughs. The first was Krueger's invention of Videoplace, a rudimentary machine that allowed two or more people to interact virtually in a 'third place'. This constituted a break from existing forms of telecommunication in that multiple people experienced a 'place' simultaneously as not being the actual world. 'People interacted within the virtual world and also with the virtual world itself' (2008: 47). The second innovation was the development of first-person perspective in videogames. Together, these two technical affordances allow SL avatars to interact with other inworld objects – including other avatars – not in a cyberspatial void but in specific virtual locations such as rooms, corridors, paths, gardens or hot-air balloons.

Nowhere is the contrast between Boellstorff's position and that of

Miller and Slater starker than on the issue of virtuality and mediation. Citing Anderson's (1983) famous example of how newspapers conveyed the idea of the modern nation as an 'imagined' or virtual community, Miller and Slater (2000: 6) conclude that 'virtuality – as the capacity of communicative technologies to constitute rather than mediate realities and to constitute relatively bounded spheres of interaction – is neither new nor specific to the Internet. Indeed, it is probably intrinsic to the process of mediation as such'. For Boellstorff, in contradistinction, although humans have always crafted themselves through culture (*homo faber*), what is new about Internet sites such as Second Life is that 'human craft ... can now create new worlds for human sociality' from within those worlds: 'I cannot meet a lover inside a novel and invite friends for a wedding ceremony there, nor can I and a group of like-minded persons buy joint property inside a television program' (Boellstorff 2008: 237).

This does not mean, however, that all Internet sites can support virtual forms of sociality and craft, says Boellstorff. For example, social network sites such as MySpace or Facebook do not qualify as virtual worlds as their significance derives – like the Trinidadian websites and chat rooms described by Miller and Slater – from 'a direct relationship to the actual world' (2008: 238). Boellstorff concludes with the cogent assertion that virtual worlds are 'distinct domains of human being' that deserve being studied on their own terms, not those of actual worlds (2008: 238). Like Hine before him (2000), he regards online ethnography as a strategy suited to certain research projects but not necessarily to others.[7]

Internet Practices and Practitioners

One remarkable feature of the development of the Internet is the sheer proliferation and diversification of its practices. All four studies further our understanding of this practical explosion by documenting and discussing actual practices in great detail. They do so, however, in rather different ways and with uneven success when it comes to their theorisation.

If Boellstorff's *Coming of Age* is firmly anchored in the synchronous practices of Bukowski and his fellow avatars, Chris Kelty's *Two Bits* is primarily a historical reconstruction of the emergence and stabilisation of the five key 'geeky' practices that make up the field of Free Software. Kelty distinguishes between four basic practices (sharing source code, conceptualising openness, applying copyright licenses, and coordinating and collaborating) and what we might call a 'meta-practice' (see Peterson 2010): the practice of arguing and discussing about the other four practices, which he terms 'the movement'.

As said earlier, Kelty regards Free Software as constituting a 'recursive public', that is, a manner of commons where geeks modify and maintain the very technological conditions of their own terms of discourse and existence. The recursive public is a manner of social imaginary (Taylor), a moral-technical understanding of social order that is partly imagined, partly concrete (as it entails computers, wires, waves, electrons, and such like).

For Kelty, Free Software is not an isolated phenomenon but part of an ongoing global reorientation of power/knowledge. This point is pursued in the final part of the book where he discusses two related non-software projects based on Free Software templates: Connexions and Creative Commons. Kelty was deeply involved with the former initiative as a mediator between the worlds of academia, software and copyright law. The aim was to produce academic textbooks in a manner similar to that of Free Software. Kelty found that his geeky 'imagination of openness ... and social order' stood him in better stead than his anthropological training. He found that Connexions managed to adapt or 'modulate' all basic Free Software practices save for the meta-practice of movement – no Free Textbook movement ensued. One major hurdle for the project's code-minded geeks was the prevalence of non-codified academic custom. In trying to 'figure out' what they were doing, project members struggled to define the finality of a scholarly work. How do such works attain identity, stability, completion? Connexions sought to redefine finality in an open, public way, with modifiability being integral to how knowledge is stabilised; but many scholars resisted this idea.

This very same question of the uneven spread and appropriation of Free Software practices into other fields of cultural production surfaces in Toni Roig's Ph.D. thesis, "Towards collaborative filmmaking" (my translation). The thesis investigates to what extent we may be moving towards more collaborative forms of filmmaking linked to the rise of Internet and other digital technologies as well as to developments such as Free Software. The case studies consist of the making of two Internet 'fan films' (by X-ILE Pictures in the United States and Energia Productions in Finland) and a Free Software-inspired film (*A Swarm of Angels* in Britain). Roig's claim to originality rests on his novel use of a practice-theoretical approach in an emerging area of Internet research (see Couldry 2004, Bräuchler and Postill 2010) to propose a typology of collaborative practices that shows great comparative potential. This 'family of practices' includes practices of production, distribution, organisation, and self-promotion as well as their (meta-pragmatic) interrelations.

Thematically, Oliver Hinkelbein's dissertation "Strategies towards the digital integration of immigrants" (my translation) takes an altogether different direction, bringing us back to one of Miller and Slater's main preoccupations: the so-called 'digital divide'. Yet Hinkelbein also pays careful attention to actual practices, in his case the practices (*Praktiken*) that make up the emergent field of 'digital integration' in Germany. His aim is to understand some of the strategies whereby both public and civic organisations seek to bridge the digital divide that reportedly separates native Germans from foreign immigrants. He does so through a multi-sited, comparative ethnographic account based on participant observation within Internet initiatives aimed at immigrants in Esslingen (public) and Hanover (civic) as well as at a number of 'expert' meetings in other locations. Although ostensibly committed to actor-network theory (ANT), the dissertation's spotlight follows the human rather than non-human agents (computers, software, networks, printers), particularly those humans who – not unlike Chris Kelty in the Connexions project – act as go-betweens across sites, technologies and constituencies.

Hinkelbein takes us through the main characteristics of each set of actors and their socio-political contexts, stressing the importance of close personal ties as well as the 'blackboxed' processes of inclusion and exclusion into networks of digital integration expertise. One crucial finding was indeed the existence of such invisible networks and their concretisation through computer clubs, mentoring sessions, seminars, and so forth. It is precisely the focus on the practices of these 'new mediators' that constitutes the study's main contribution to a strangely neglected area of research: Internet technologies and grassroots leadership in contexts of socioeconomic development. New mediators face the challenge of having to recruit and mobilise other social actors in pursuit of their goals whilst surviving financially in the fiercely competitive market of grassroots ICT initiatives. The upshot is a relentless drive for creative innovation.

Conceptual Work

In a relatively new interdisciplinary field such as Internet Studies in which, as we saw earlier, conceptual muddles are common, the rigorous conceptual work undertaken in all four studies stands out. These conceptual efforts take two main forms: (a) clearing the conceptual ground around the study's main Internet formation (especially in Boellstorff and Kelty), and (b) broadening the existing conceptual lexicon around the chosen Internet research area (more noticeably in Roig and Hinkelbein).

Both Kelty and Boellstorff are at pains to clarify what their respective objects of Internet study are *not* so that they can proceed to elucidate what they actually are. Thus Kelty explains that Free Software is not a collective, an informal organisation, a crowd, or even a social movement. Rather, as said earlier, it is an Internet-mediated 'recursive public', a new kind of public sphere in which operating systems and social systems are inextricably entwined. Similarly, Boellstorff explains that although Second Life may approximate some elements of reality for purposes of immersion, it is not a simulation (i.e., it is not 'virtual reality'); nor is it a social network site comparable to Facebook or MySpace but rather a *place*, neither is it a posthuman realm (in fact, it makes us more human) nor a sensational world of wild cybersex and rampant consumerism as portrayed by the news media (instead, mundane daily practices are the norm).

For their part, both Roig and Hinkelbein guide their readers with great aplomb through a number of semantic minefields that lie at the heart of contemporary Internet Studies. Roig carefully unpacks important but often muddled notions such as 'new media', 'cultural producers', 'digital filmmaking' and 'audiences'. He successfully manages to develop a set of working definitions of key terms in the first half of the thesis that he then applies to the empirical materials in the second half. Likewise, Hinkelbein expends considerable energy sharpening a set of conceptual tools that he helpfully lists in a glossary (e.g., 'blackboxing', 'digital integration', 'new mediator', 'translation').

Epochal Claims

In the final part of *Coming of Age*, Tom Boellstorff makes an epochal forecast based on his Second Life research. He argues that SL and other virtual worlds may herald the advent of a new age driven not by information or knowledge (as technology authors have told us for half a century) but by craft or *techne*, as exemplified by SL residents' keen dedication to crafting their own world and its virtual artefacts. Instead of the promised Information Age or Knowledge Society, suggests Boellstorff, we may be heading towards the Age of Techne.

This is a questionable prognosis. In fact, the evidence and arguments presented in *Coming of Age* demonstrate that SL is a highly specific Internet environment that is markedly distinct from sites devoted to online games, social networking, blogging, bookmarking, micro-blogging, discussing, and so on, where crafting is not a salient feature. To return to Miller and Slater's Trinidad argument, what all four studies capture is not a totalising epochal 'logic' but rather ever more differentiated Internet 'technologies, practices, contexts' (2000: 3). The evidence provided in the reviewed texts strongly suggests that the Internet – and indeed the world – is becoming ever more plural and that no universal 'logic of practice' (not even the logic of *techne*) is gaining ascendancy at the expense of all other logics. Second Life has found its own niche within an Internet ecology that is expanding dramatically as millions of new users join and myriad new platforms and applications are fashioned every year. This is an Internet niche that attracts, like all niches, certain kinds of people but not others. As someone who suffers from acute time poverty, I for one could only become an active SL resident if I turned such participation into a research project. Even many Internet users with time on their hands and valid credit cards will find no compelling reason to join SL, opting instead for other platforms. Such refusenik stances point to yet another Internet question worthy of further investigation.

Positioning this Study

Localizing the Internet seeks to contribute to the existing anthropological literature on the Internet in a number of ways. First, like Hinkelbein (2008) I engage with highly localized Internet projects aimed at people who the authorities regards as being in need of digital support. Indeed, Hinkelbein and I were both part of the same comparative project (see Preface and Strauss 2007). There is a clear difference, however, between our studies. In Hinkelbein's case, the beneficiaries of public monies were foreign immigrants in Germany who were deemed to be on the wrong side of the 'digital divide'. By contrast, my Subang Jaya mentors were mostly Internet-savvy, middle-class nationals (albeit largely from the ethnic Chinese minority) who the federal authorities hoped would be an 'e-Governance' role-model to the rest of the country (Chapter 4). One frequent complaint in the suburb where I conducted fieldwork was that it was the local authorities themselves who were unable to keep abreast of residents' Internet progress! Therefore, this is most emphatically not a digital divide study.

A second intended contribution of this book to the anthropological Internet corpus is methodological. Whilst participant observation is as central to the present study as it is in existing monographs, in the chapters that follow I add a diachronic (or historical) dimension to this synchronic approach (see Postill 2009). Like Kelty (2008) in his study of Free Software geeks, I have delved deep into the online archives of the social universe under study – with the notable difference that Subang Jaya's archives go no further back than 1999. This historical dimension allows me in subsequent chapters and in the Conclusion to reconstruct the structuring of a very specific kind of Internet field: Subang Jaya's field of residential affairs, a domain of practice that is becoming ever more mediated by Internet technologies. In short, this is an account that unfolds over a period of ten years, from 1999 to 2009.

Third, like my foregoers, I too pay careful attention to conceptual matters. This is especially important when working with people in the field who are technically and politically sophisticated. Thus although I sometimes follow everyday Malaysian English usages to present the empirical materials, I also take pains to distinguish folk from anthropological terms in order to avoid vague or confusing formulations. For example, I retain the notion of 'community' as an emotive folk notion commonly used in Malaysia but being careful not to use this notoriously imprecise term to refer to actual social formations, for the reasons explained earlier. One effective way to loosen the hold of community and network as the paradigmatic Internet Studies notions is to broaden our sociological/anthropological lexicon. In the present study I carry out such broadening in two main directions: first, by fashioning or borrowing field-theoretical notions such as 'field of residential affairs', 'Internet field', 'social field', 'social drama', 'field law', 'arena' and 'action-set'; second, by conceiving of sociality as being inherently plural and context-dependent (Jean-Klein 2003, Amit and Rapport 2002) rather than in the overly general terms that we find in the existing Internet literature, e.g., 'community sociality' vs. 'network sociality' (Wittel 2001, see this volume, Chapter 7).

Notes

1. See Chigona (2006), Davies (2004), Day (2001, 2005), Dutta-Bergman (2005), Ferlander and Timms (2001), Foth (2004a, 2004b), Gurstein et al. (2003), Keeble and Loader (2001), Kubicek and Wagner (2002), Pigg (2001), Pinkett (2003), Schuler (1996, 2000), Shearman (1999), Stillman and Stoecker (2005); for reviews of this literature see Loader and Keeble (2004), Pigg and Crank (2004), and Taylor (2004).
2. Two rare pieces on local ICT initiatives that go beyond the community/network paradigm are Venkatesh (2003) and Agar et al. (2002).
3. http://listserv.aoir.org/pipermail/air-l-aoir.org/2006-August/010366.html
4. I thank an anonymous reader for posing this question which has helped me think through these issues.
5. A variant of field theory is being used as the theoretical thrust by a media research group at Goldsmiths College, University of London – see http://www.goldsmiths.ac.uk/media-research-programme
6. Personal communication from Alexander T. Smith (22 May 2006) who independently coined the term 'banal activism' after anthropological fieldwork

among Conservative Party activists in Scotland.

7. For some enlightening, and at times heated, debates on these matters, see the EASA Media Anthropology e-seminar "Researching the internet", 27 September to 4 October 2005 (http://www.media-anthropology.net/braeuchler_eseminar.pdf) and a discussion of *Coming of Age* with its author on the anthropological blog Savage Minds entitled "Ethnography of the Virtual", 12 June 2008 (http://savageminds.org/2008/06/12/ethnography-of-the-virtual/).

CHAPTER 3

Research Setting

Subang Jaya is a largely middle-class suburb in the Klang Valley

Goh Ban Lee (2004)

Subang Jaya, 11 May 2003. We meet at the train station, as previously agreed over email. I recognise him from the Web: Jeff Ooi, the owner of the Subang Jaya e-Community Portal and since January a rising star among Malaysia's political bloggers. We exchange informal greetings and walk up towards the nearby Carrefour shopping mall. Jeff asks me how long I have been in Malaysia. I tell him that on this occasion just over a week but that I have been in Peninsular Malaysia a number of times before. I also tell him about my eighteen months of fieldwork in the eastern state of Sarawak studying media uses among the Iban. After mentioning his own Sarawak experience, he asks me how I got here from Bangi, on the far side of the new federal capital, Putrajaya. I tell him that I took a taxi from the UKM campus where I am staying. He says it must have been an expensive trip. I confirm this but provide no figure for fear of sounding like a tourist who has just been taken for a ride. I add that I couldn't face the long detour via Kuala Lumpur's central station after yesterday's rail travel collapse following heavy storms.

We enter a small Starbucks café inside the mall. The tables' surfaces are chessboards. Some have pieces on them, others are bare. Jeff picks a table by the window but I ask if we can choose one free of chess pieces so I can take notes. He has no objections. His mobile phone rings. I ask him what I can get him but he quickly says something like "Oh, no, it's okay, this is my turf; I'll do the honours". I thank him as we are joined by KW Chang who co-administers the online forum with Jeff. They both give me their business cards. I apologise for not being able to reciprocate but Chang says it doesn't matter, as there are a lot of them but only me, so for them remembering my name will be easier. We all laugh.

Chang has heard that they have a new iced tea at Starbucks worth trying so I order it as well. I reintroduce myself as Jeff comes back with the drinks. "As I was saying to Jeff ..." and tell them that I am in Malaysia to study local e-Government and e-Community projects as part of a comparative research project with other researchers working in the UK, Germany and the Netherlands. I then explain briefly, by way of example, the kind of research that Paul Strauss (2007) is about to conduct in the London borough of Newham. Jeff asks whether Newham is a top-down or bottom-up project. I reply it looks like a top-down project set in a poor multiethnic neighbourhood, but we'll have to wait and see as Strauss hasn't yet begun fieldwork. Jeff explains that most Subang Jaya residents are working class. Perhaps I look surprised because he then asks what we mean in Britain by 'working class'. Caught unprepared, I improvise an account of class in terms of cultural capital that you acquire mostly from your family, school and peers. Despite the reported blurring of class boundaries in recent decades, I continue, there are still important distinctions between the classes. To this, Jeff says that although a majority of Subang Jaya residents may wear white collars and work from 9 to 5, they are still workers.

We then move on to the interview proper. Having gone through their online archives, I have a list of eighteen points to cover. The first question concerns the history of their local Web portal. Jeff starts by helpfully sketching the history of Subang Jaya. We are now sitting in the older part of the municipality. Built in the 1970s it lies north of what is now the Shah Alam expressway (E5). The area south of the expressway is known as USJ; it was built later, in the 1980s and 1990s. Whilst in the north there are a growing number of retired residents, USJ residents like my interviewees are generally younger, Internet-savvy, and white collar. "Marketing people love our profile," says Jeff, "they call us PMEBs: professionals, managers, executives and businessmen."

****

As is common with ethnographic tales of entry, this vignette raises a host of questions. For the sake of brevity, in this chapter I take up just three of them, namely the geographical setting of the present study, the class and ethno-religious position of the majority of residents, and the methodology adopted in the study. Whilst concurring with Goh Ban Lee (2004) that Subang Jaya is best characterised as a 'middle-class' and not (*pace* Jeff Ooi) 'working-class' suburb in the Klang Valley, below I seek to unpack and contextualise this problematic notion within the particularities of Subang Jaya and Malaysia.

The Klang Corridor

In 1859 Kuala Lumpur was little more than a collection of huts occupied by immigrant tin miners from China. By 1896 it had become the new capital of the Federated Malayan States and a transport hub, and by the 1930s it was a racially segregated British colonial town surrounded by rubber plantations. The satellite township of Petaling Jaya, in the Klang Valley, was built in 1953. Originally intended to relocate squatters, eventually suburban homes were built for an embryonic population of middle-class commuters (Dick and Rimmer 2003: 325; Thong 1995: 318). Kuala Lumpur only came into its own as a major urban centre when Singapore seceded from the newly created Malaysian Federation in 1965. Overnight it became not only the largest city in the Federation but also a focal point of Malay, and later Malaysian, nationalism. A construction frenzy ensued in an effort to bolster this newly acquired status through modern architecture. Meanwhile, where formerly the transport infrastructure had served a colonial economy based on the export of tin and rubber, the newly independent nation sought to put its transport policy at the service of nation-building (Senbil et al. 2009).

In the 1970s and 1980s Malaysia underwent a prodigious economic transformation. It went from being an agricultural and mining economy to a regional manufacturing centre, with direct foreign investment accounting for up to 50 per cent of all new investments in manufacturing (Thong 1995). The Klang corridor running from Kuala Lumpur to Port Klang was consolidated in the post-independence years, blessed with both a rail and road link which fostered rapid industrialisation. Yet regional planners soon recognised the need for a second corridor. As a result in 1975 the university town of Bangi – where I stayed at the beginning of fieldwork – was created, served by its own rail and road link.

The notion of 'corridor' has remained central to federal government economic planning throughout. Thus in the Industrial Master Plan of 1986–1995, the government prioritised the industrialisation of Peninsular Malaysia's western corridor, that is, the west coast. This region required far less investment than the east coast which has remained underdeveloped (Thong 1995). More recently, this same idea has been applied to Malaysia's efforts to emulate California's Silicon Valley with the creation of the Multimedia Super Corridor to the south of Kuala Lumpur (see Chapter 4).

Industrialisation was accompanied by a population explosion. As the industries spread further away from Kuala Lumpur, they soaked up rural populations, with an abundant pool of low-cost female labour as an added incentive (Ong 1987). Today the Kuala Lumpur metropolitan region has a population of about three million and could be developing into a 'mega-urban region' covering the entire Klang Valley (Mohamad and Kiggundu 2007, McGee and Robinson 1995). A recent study comparing the Kuala Lumpur region and the Kei-Han-Shin metropolitan area in Japan is revealing (Senbil et al. 2009). While the average age of the population was 41.3 years in Kei-Han-Shin, it was significantly lower (30.3) in Kuala Lumpur, a population marked by 'school-age cohorts' rather than baby boomers reaching retirement age as in the Japanese case. This contrast is captured in the unemployment figures for both regions, with Kuala Lumpur having a significantly smaller proportion of retired individuals (3.18 per cent vs. 17.3 per cent) and homemakers (4.77 per cent vs. 16.8 per cent) among the jobless. A further notable contrast is in evidence in the average household size, with Kuala Lumpur's average of 4.2 persons being much larger than Kei-Han-Shin's 2.84 persons (Senbil et al. 2009).

The region's extraordinary rate of economic growth has come, however, at a high environmental and social cost (Terinam et al. 2009). The policy of favouring corridor development meant a lack of integration of the various corridors. Thus plans to create a mass transit system modelled on Singapore's never materialised, and the official dream of public transport carrying 40 per cent of passengers is today seen as 'wishful thinking' (Dick and Rimmer 2003). Some observers point at the collusion between the car industry and other industries such as oil, rubber, steel and insurance (Mohamad and Kiggundu 2007), or blame Malaysia's former prime minister, Dr Mahathir, for lavishing resources on the 'national car' instead of pursuing a long-term public transport strategy (Sim 2006). Transport scholars fear that the region could face an 'intractable traffic crisis' unless private car ownership is curtailed and public transport is dramatically overhauled (Barter 2004). A related problem is the ongoing suburbanisation which leaves in its wake a declining inner-city population as those who can afford it out-migrate along the regional corridor clusters that stretch from Kuala Lumpur to Port Klang (Siong 2008, Terinam et al. 2009).

All this has led some to describe the region as a miniature Los Angeles: a low-density, car-dependent urban sprawl that is worlds apart from the clean and orderly Singapore-like conurbation once envisaged by planners (Dick and Rimmer 2003).

Subang Jaya and USJ

Subang Jaya and USJ form a largely middle-income suburb of Kuala Lumpur located in the Klang Valley, Selangor State. Much of the territory was once a plantation, initially devoted to rubber and later to cocoa and palm oil. Estnerie s/o Thamotaran, a resident of what today is USJ 2, was a field supervisor from 1960 until his early retirement in 1991. He recalls life on the estate as being pleasantly regulated – a cyclical alternation of fieldwork, office work, religious practice and leisure. In the racially strati-fied world of the plantation, this Malayalee Indian mediated between the British (later Malay and Chinese) management and the Tamil workers. He was the chairman of the Hindu temples, and sent his children to a mission school in Klang. The workers, in contrast, sent theirs to the plantation's Tamil school. Entertainment was provided by itinerant cinema companies that brought to the plantation popular Tamil films. 'The British were very strict,' he told me, 'we had few gangsters'.[1]

In the 1970s, the close-knit plantation world began to unravel as Sub-ang Jaya was opened up to housing developments. Covering an area of 583 hectares, it became the largest township in South East Asia developed by a single private company, the Malaysian conglomerate Sime Darby Bhd.[2] Early residents recall that very few people in those days were willing to move to the area, as it was perceived to be 'out there in the *hutan* (jungle)'. At the time there was but a single coffee shop and few retail outlets. There were also rumours that aircraft landing at Subang Airport often unloaded their unused fuel on the houses below. Given this strong reticence, the develop-ers began to offer semi-furnished houses at very competitive prices.[3]

Eventually the market took off, with USJ opening up in 1988 and developing very rapidly to meet the demands of largely middle-class families, many of them ethnic Chinese. By 1999 Subang Jaya had twelve thousand residential units, where USJ had thirty-seven thousand units spread over 728 hectares and was still expanding but was reaching satu-ration point.[4] Because of their staggered settlement, each half has a dis-tinctive demographic and domestic cycle profile. Subang Jaya's families have as a norm older children than those in USJ. At the time of field-work in 2003–2004 many offspring were already in their twenties and even thirties, and no longer lived with their parents. By contrast, many USJ families still had children of preschool or school age.

As the suburb bourgeoned, the Tamil estate workers were made redun-dant and offered subsidised flats from which they had to find new jobs. When the available land grew scarce, several Hindu temples were bulldozed to give way to housing estates. Protests by local Hindus, although amply covered in the Tamil press and on the residents' site USJ.com.my, were ineffectual.[5]

When USJ reached saturation the suburban expansion moved to out-ly-ing areas such as Seri Kembangan and Puchong. The latter was originally settled by Orang Asli (aborigines) and Malays, followed in colonial times by Punjabi cattle ranchers, Tamil rubber tappers and Chinese tin miners.[6] While Subang Jaya and USJ were built by a single developer, Puchong residents faced huge challenges as numerous developers – reportedly as many as thirty to sixty – were operating in the area in the mid-2000s. Com-plaints about lack of adequate planning and coordination were rife, and would be sometimes reported in the *Malay Mail* and other local news-papers. As my field research focused on Subang Jaya and especially USJ where most of the Internet activism is concentrated, in the remainder of the book I will only make passing mention of Puchong.

Everyday Life

The lives of most adult residents of USJ revolve around work and family. Many men and women commute by car to workplaces located elsewhere in the Klang Valley. With the growing volume of traffic and the inadequate public transport alternatives, this is for many an unpleasant daily chore, and one that frequently features in conversation. Those fortunate residents who do not need to commute – many of them elderly or very young – have time to exercise or play in the small greens (*padang*) and along leafy streets at the crack of dawn, before the humid heat becomes unbearable. During the day, it is common to see foreign maids going about their daily round of activities while their employers are away at work. The greens and playgrounds will be busy again before dusk, when the temperatures are more tolerable and many commuters will have returned home from their workplaces.

The pressures of juggling work and family are severe, and they are often remarked upon by local residents. Thus a USJ 6 resident told me that 'here everybody minds their own business: you go to work, come back, make sure the kids are well fed'. He lamented the infrequency of community gatherings and the fact that 'sometimes neighbours don't even smile at you'. Similarly, a local doctor half-joked at a public gather-ing about the demographic consequences of dual-career lifestyles: 'Our problem here is that many people are taking care of the rice bowl. How often do they have sexual intercourse? They have no time, as they both come back home very tired from work. So how are they going to have children?'. Another local resident told me that neighbours generally do not trust one another and that people will often move into an area where they have friends or relations. Her own neighbourly relations soured over an overgrown tree. On one occasion I even had to hurry to her aid as she was alone at home and fearful of her increasingly abusive next-door neighbour. Matters were compounded by their different racial and religious backgrounds and by her neighbour's political connections.

When local residents are not at work or asleep one popular site of leisure and consumption is the shopping mall. The most venerable of all is Subang Parade, reputed as being Malaysia's longest mall and the first to be built in the township (in 1988). Malls are much more than places to shop; they are key loci of suburban sociality, air-conditioned havens where Subang Jaya residents can escape the heat and spend time and money on a large range of activities, from shopping, eating and drinking to bowling, playing computer games, going to the cinema, exercising in a gym or just *lepak-ing* ('doing nothing'). Recognising their social centrality, the municipal council (MPSJ), police force, and political class regularly use shopping malls for their outreach programmes. Other popular leisure pursuits include entertaining at home, practising sports, attending birthday parties and weddings, shopping at hypermarkets such as Giant, Tesco or Carrefour, or visiting a 'traditional' night market (*pasar malam*).

Ethno-religious Divides

In 2001 the Subang Jaya municipality as a whole had a population ranging between 423,000 and 470,000.[7] The official figures for Subang Jaya's racial breakdown also show a significant discrepancy. Thus, while one account, for 2001, reads 45 percent Chinese, 40 per cent Malays, and 15 per cent Indians and 'Others' – predominantly immigrant workers from poorer Asian countries – another, for 1998, speaks of 60 per cent Chinese, 25 per cent Malays, and 15 per cent Indians and 'Others', just three years before.[8] My own personal observations incline me towards the latter breakdown.

Whatever the exact percentages, these ethno-religious divides shape everyday and seasonal practices, from sharing a meal to practising a sport to performing daily rituals or going on holiday. Thus in the local area where I lived, USJ 6, evening sports followed broad ethnic lines. Whilst most basketball players were Chinese, Indians preferred football (soccer) and Malays *sepak takraw*, an indigenous game played with a small rattan ball.[9] Efforts by local politicians, council staff and residents to promote interethnic youth sports must be understood against these entrenched divisions (see Chapter 4).

Another popular evening activity in (sub)urban Malaysia is eating out. There is no shortage of food in Subang Jaya–USJ, from road stalls and fast food outlets to cafés, coffee shops, food courts and restaurants.

While fast food outlets such as KFC or Burger King, cafes such as Star-bucks, and *mamak* stalls operated by Tamil Muslims cater to all ethno-religious groups, other establishments occupy clearly defined ethnic niches with distinctive cultural markers and social scripts. Thus in Ma-lay eateries the food is frequently served hot on the counter, the staff's manner is usually gentle and courteous (*sopan*), no alcohol or pork are served, and the bill is settled at the end of the meal. By contrast, Chinese eateries pay less attention to ambience and more to food quality and taste, the bill is normally settled upfront, and the waiters' manner may strike a foreign visitor as being unfriendly, even curt at times.

Islam is a key divider. As Fischer (2001) has argued, Malay middle-class families form their identities partly through the complex interplay of Islamic beliefs and 'Western' consumption practices, some of which may be banned or come under close scrutiny for their possible un-Islam-ic nature. Thus while in Chinese-dominated Subang Jaya and USJ pubs and bars are ubiquitous, in neighbouring Shah Alam, with its majority Malay (Muslim) population, drinking alcohol is only permitted in beer factories and certain hotels. Malay men from Shah Alam and further afield are said to patronise the Subang Jaya bars illegally. Some of these establishments hire young hostesses – many of them immigrant workers – who are entrusted with replenishing the patrons' drinks and may, in some cases, offer sexual services as well.

The near-ban on alcohol imposed by the Shah Alam authorities is part of an Islamising trend across Malaysia that has gathered pace since the 1980s (King and Wilder 2003). In the 1960s and early 1970s, for mid-dle-class Malay hosts to serve alcohol to their guests was regarded as a sign of modern sophistication, and many homes even had bars fitted in for this purpose. With Islamisation, however, guests today are more likely to share with their hosts recitations from the Qur'an than alcoholic beverages. The government's strategy against fundamentalist groups has been, as in other spheres of governance, a combination of repression and accom-modation. Thus in the late 1970s and 1980s a number of Islamist leaders were arrested without trial under the country's draconian Internal Secu-rity Act (ISA) while the government redoubled its 'moderate' Islamisa-tion efforts (Crouch 1996: 244–45). For example, during the early stages of my fieldwork in 2003, Subang Jaya's main mosque was identified as a stronghold of the opposition Islamist party PAS and it was reported that the ruling party, UMNO, was struggling to 'win it over'.[10]

Interestingly, from the 1970s there has been a parallel trend among Malaysian Chinese away from the old establishment churches and to-wards newer fundamentalist Pentecostal and charismatic churches. A study by Judith Nagata in the northern city of Penang revealed a strong growth of Pentecostal-charismatic churches, particularly among English-educated Chinese professionals and their families. As has been observed in other countries, many were 'born again' during a major life crisis (Nagata 1995, see also Dahles 2007). Although no statistics are available on the size of charismatic congregations in Subang Jaya, local residents told me that they have mushroomed in recent years. As Dahles (2007) has found, these churches operate at the interface between business and religion. Like Judith Nagata in her Penang research, I was struck during Sunday services by the mixture of business acumen ('aggressive tithing'), showbiz, charisma and social work. The Sunday gatherings were services in more than one sense: they not only served Jesus, but also provided valuable social services (e.g., free crèches) as well as places to network with other residents and socialise with one's peers (such as other parents, teenagers, children, maids).

While it is important to stress the activities of Christians and Muslims, we should not lose sight of other religious organisations catering for Subang Jaya's middle classes. Thus, Buddhist groups operating in the township have adapted some ideas and practices from the charismatic Christians (e.g., playing guitars, reading the scriptures, born-again testimonies, a stress on success in business), an international phenomenon described as 'the churching of Buddhism' (Nagata 1995). I observed this trend firsthand at a shopping mall in USJ where a Taiwan-based Buddhist organisation owns a bookshop and vegetarian café and regularly organises events aimed at the Mandarin-educated middle classes.

The Middle Classes

> The newly affluent in emerging markets echo the tastes of the English middle class 150 years ago. They want travel, improved health services, private schools and better public infrastructure. Like the Victorians, they are also keen on self-improvement.
>
> *The Economist* (2009: 8)

As mentioned above, the local governance scholar Goh Ban Lee has described Subang Jaya as 'a largely middle-class suburb in the Klang Valley'. But what and who exactly is 'the middle class'? Or should that be 'the middle *classes*'? How useful is this notoriously fuzzy and contested notion? These are questions that Malaysian and other Asia-Pacific scholars have long debated but remain unresolved (see Embong 2000 and 2002, Gomez 2004, Jomo 2000, Jones 1998, Kahn 1996, Kessler 2001, Shiraishi 2006, So 2006). Fortunately, a recent study of 'the new mid-

middle classes' in the developing world published in *The Economist* clears a path through the conceptual thicket. The broad features of the new middle classes identified by *The Economist* match closely those of Subang Jaya's majority population.

First, this is a class of people that enjoys, by Malaysian standards, 'a reasonable amount of discretionary income'. In other words, a majority of Subang Jaya-USJ residents 'do not live from hand to mouth, job to job, season to season, as the poor do' (*The Economist* 2009: 3; see also Embong 2000). When Malaysia's official household income and facilities census was featured in *The Edge* magazine on 10 July 2008, it triggered a lively discussion on Subang Jaya's main online forum under the thread title 'Half of M'sian households earn below 3,000 ringgit a month!' (c. 850 US dollars). The reaction from KW Chang, the forum moderator we met in the ethnographic vignette that opens this chapter, gives us a clue as to what counts as a 'reasonable' minimum income among Subang Jaya's middle classes:

> Earning below RM3K per month is a real challenge if you live within big cities, especially in the Klang Valley. I take my hat off to all in that category who are pulling through on 3K or less per month. What we need to know is HOW they are making it possible to survive on a monthly household income of RM3K or less.[11]

According to a May 2007 study commissioned by the shopping mall Subang Parade, the average household income of Subang Jaya-USJ residents was nearly three times that benchmark figure at 8,627 ringgits (over 2,400 US dollars), while an exit survey of Subang Parade shoppers yielded an even higher average of 9,238 ringgits per month (2,600 US dollars).[12] Ten years earlier, in 1997, the municipal council estimated Subang Jaya's average monthly household income to be an unspecified 'higher' figure than that for the state of Selangor as a whole (4,006 ringgits). In stark contrast, the national average was at the time 2,606 ringgits.[13] At the time of writing (August 2009) this portrait of relative affluence must, however, be set against the current global economic crisis and the reported 'soaring cost of living in the Klang Valley'. Thus a 28 February 2009 article in *The Star* reported that Malaysia's consumer price index (CPI) increased 3.9 per cent in January 2009 in relation to the same month a year earlier, with non-alcoholic beverages and food up 9.8 per cent and an interviewee reporting that a Klang Valley resident now requires 15 to 20 ringgits for three daily meals.[14]

Second, on the whole Subang Jaya's adult residents are in 'regular, formal employment' (*The Economist* 2009: 3; cf. Embong 2000, Jomo 2000). The Subang Parade study found that approximately 70 per cent of their shoppers were in what we might call upper- and middle-income types of employment, ranging from professionals and CEOs to office administrators and marketing personnel. In addition 16.1 per cent were university students and 8.2 per cent were housewives. Assuming that a majority of the housewives also belong to middle- or high-income households, we can estimate that around 90 per cent of shoppers are middle- or high-income by Malaysian standards.

Third, Subang Jaya's middle-class residents are accustomed to abstracting away from the specific details of other people's personalities and backgrounds 'in order to get something done' (*The Economist* 2009: 5). Thus during the early stages of fieldwork I was surprised by how little reference ethnic Chinese residents made to other residents' subethnic backgrounds (e.g., Hokkien, Hakka, Cantonese), or indeed to their places of origin. This contrasted sharply with my prior experience among rural Iban in Sarawak who, like me, enjoyed nothing more than discerning in great detail differences in dialect, accent, and custom among Iban hailing from different river basins. Instead, in Subang Jaya the emphasis was very much on the here-and-now of a busy metropolitan existence, or on imminent travel plans to other parts of the country or abroad. This letter to the online newspaper *Malaysiakini* exemplifies how most Subang Jaya Chinese view their intra-ethnic differences:

> The Chinese of yesteryears had minute microscopic ethnic markers, whether you are a Lim, Lee or Tan or Goh for that matter. To complicate these markers, you have Teo Chews and Hokkiens and Cantonese and so on and so forth. Then you have the Foo Chows amongst the Hokkiens and then the Hin Huas, Eng Choons and so forth … Overtime, the Chinese saw that fighting with one's brother-in-law to protect someone else's commercial and monetary interest was stupid and only for the ignoramus … Today the Chinese are largely homogenous, no longer divided along the fault lines of old. They have learned to be interdependent and support each other.[15]

An important qualification is in order, however, with regard to *inter*ethnic relations. While relations among ethnic Chinese, Indian and white middle-class residents were in my experience generally smooth and sustained, when it came to the Malays the situation was more complicated. This was in part on account of the religious and legal interdictions mentioned earlier, which among other things greatly restrict the Malays' opportunities for socialising at night with other ethnic groups. As the author of the *Malaysiakini* letter rightly puts it, 'ethnic markers in modern Malaysia are over the same words [as they were in ancient China] – honor, dignity and clanship, [only now] under the guise of 'bangsa', 'bahasa', and 'Tuhan' [race, language, and God]'.

Fourth, like middle-class parents everywhere, Subang Jaya's parents are 'committed to education' and have no economic need to 'take their children out of school to work in the fields or in a sweatshop' (*The Economist* 2009: 9). Schooling and education were a constant topic of conversation and source of anxiety among the parents I met in the suburb. Unfavourable comparisons were often made with Australia and other Western countries and there was great frustration with what were regarded as the declining standards of state schools in Malaysia. One way out of this predicament was home schooling, a trend that appeared to be gathering pace at the time of the fieldwork, especially among Chinese Christians concerned about the seeming Islamisation of the school system. Another perpetual source of bitterness was the stringent university quotas which effectively bar most non-Malay students from entering the state universities, forcing ethnic Chinese and Indian parents to pay privately for a university education at home or overseas.

Finally, although a typically middle-class 'gift for entrepreneurship' (*The Economist* 2009: 10) is clearly in evidence in Subang Jaya – as we shall see in subsequent chapters when discussing the 'social entrepreneurship' of leading Internet activists – of greater resonance to the Malaysian case is the perceptive observation that around the developing world, '[a] middle class that has grown largely to tend to the state will behave differently from one that is based on the private sector'. It is primarily in this sense that we can speak of Subang Jaya's middle 'classes'. One fundamental feature of the Malaysian polity is that while the government service is the virtual monopoly of the Malays and other 'indigenous' (*Bumiputra*) groups, the private sector is still largely in the hands of the Chinese, despite decades of affirmative action aimed at creating a new class of Malay entrepreneurs. A perfect example of this ethno-sectoral chasm is Subang Jaya's municipal council (MPSJ), a manner of native reservation surrounded by a largely non-Malay population. On entering this palatial building, employees and visitors alike enter not only a site of state power, but also a strongly marked Malay and Muslim cultural space. On exiting they find themselves once again, as it were, in the 'private sector' of Malaysia's racialised geography, more 'Chinaburb' than Chinatown.[16] In sum, although it is fair to say that the middle classes are unavoidably embedded in a 'state-market power matrix' (Kahn 1996: 25), in the Malaysian case we must stress the extremely uneven distribution of the two main ethnic groups across the public–private sector divide.

With all its merits, *The Economist's* survey downplays two chief characteristics of the middle classes. One is the significant cultural differences that exist between the middle classes of different countries, even within the same geographical region. I have argued elsewhere (Postill, 2006)

2006) that Malaysia is far more than an 'imagined community' (Anderson 1983). In fact, Malaysia is a *culture area* that has its own "named human population which shares myths and memories, a mass public culture, a designated homeland [and] economic unity" but is far from having achieved, as we have just seen, "equal rights and duties for all members" (Smith 1995: 56–57). Like Bourdieu's France (1984, 1998), Malaysia is what Gellner (1983) would term a 'cultural space' in which human agents and groups continually readjust their relative positions to one another within that overall space. One way of doing this is through consumption practices that index one's possession of certain amounts of economic, cultural and other forms of capital, e.g., holidaying abroad. These practices are not only rewarding in their own right (see Warde 2005), they also tell fellow Malaysians how well one is doing 'along the path to prosperity' – to recall an old governmental slogan on television (Postill 2006: 194). Although many of these consumption practices are imported (e.g., drinking coffee at Starbucks, shopping at Tesco, watching a Honk Kong DVD), others are home-grown (e.g., visiting a wet market, eating at a *mamak* stall). More importantly, it is (a) the assemblage of Malaysian and imported cultural materials and (b) their embedding in a mass public culture that together constitute the country's cultural uniqueness and distinguish it from neighbouring culture areas such as Singapore or Indonesia (Postill 2006: 193).

This pan-Malaysian public culture relies on two thoroughly entangled dominant languages: English and Malay. With varying degrees of flair and confidence, most middle-class Subang Jaya residents are at least competent, and often fluent, in both languages (although many residents struggle with Malay officialese). When spouses speak two different Chinese 'dialects', English will often become the main family language and the children's mother tongue.

In her studies of language uses in Malaysian business settings, Nair-Venugopal (2000, 2003) found '"un-English" intonation patterns and syllable time rhythm' as well as a number of ethnic sub-variants of Malaysian English (ME) corresponding with speakers' native languages. She also found a high frequency of code-mixing of Malay and English as well as code-switching into Malay. My experience was rather different. Because I was participating (both online and offline) mostly in Chinese-majority settings with few Malay interlocutors, I found far less code-switching and code-mixing than Nair-Venugopal and an overwhelming predominance of fairly standard ME. I did, however, find that English-educated speakers would at times playfully switch to a lower-class sub-variant of ME in order to display their own linguistic capital at the expense of less sophisticated speakers.

The second middle-class feature de-emphasized by *The Economist*'s writers is a strong class awareness – an awareness of being neither rich nor poor, of being 'just middle class folks trying to make a decent living' (see below). This awareness is continually reproduced in Subang Jaya in a range of contexts and media. One frequent gripe is the common misperception of the suburb as the preserve of 'rich people'. Thus in April 2009, following the reported kidnapping of a boy in the neighbouring suburb of Bandar Utama (BU), a Subang Jaya resident wrote on the local online forum: 'I dunno, seems the last I heard of kidnapping in SJ/USJ was the kid in SS19. BU & SJ/USJ are popular areas for this kind of activity. A lot of people mistaken these 2 areas as rich people community whereas we are all just middle class folks trying to make a decent living in an honest way. tsk tsk tsk …'[17]

In a country that is famously 'title-crazy' (*gila gelaran*), the antics of wealthy Malaysians with honorific titles (e.g., *Tun, Tan Sri, Datuk, Dato', Datin*) were a constant source of conversation and merriment among Subang Jaya's middle classes. Besides the social status and glamour carried by a title, 'it also opens doors to business opportunities and other pecuniary benefits'.[18] Particularly amusing was the seeming proliferation of such titles as well as the frequent rumours about individuals who had allegedly purchased theirs on the market.

An even more frequent subject of conversation during fieldwork concerned not the upper but the lower classes. For dual-career parents reliant on foreign workers for their household chores and childcare, maids were good not only 'to think with' but also good to worry about. Stories of maids (many of them Indonesian) who had sexual relations with their male employers, or bewitched them so they could elope together, of maids who ran off with the gardener and the family silver, of maids who abused their young charges, of maids who were themselves abused by their employers, of Christian employers reluctant to employ a Muslim maid, and so on, were the stuff of everyday suburban conversation and a news media staple.

Take the story of the rich expatriate and the wronged maid that I was told by a Subang Jaya resident in September 2003. Not long ago, a maid in a provincial capital was falsely accused by another maid (who was the married expat's lover) of stealing a diamond ring from her. Arrested by the police, she would have been raped while in custody had her husband not begged for mercy outside the police station. A few days later, the concubine discovered the ring in a bin and informed her white lover. He advised her to drop the charges and the wronged maid was freed but was never told the reason. She sought legal advice yet could not find it locally so she travelled to distant Kuala Lumpur where she found a lawyer who succeeded in settling with the expatriate out of court. The lawyer also wrote to his bosses in his home country and he was dismissed. The story was never reported in the press.

Maids are caught in the bind of being seen to erode the very family-building foundations they were hired to firm up. Sometimes this perceived threat will be communicated in the form of emailed or posted jokes. For instance, an inappropriately lewd joke was posted to a Subang Jaya mailing list about a little girl who finally discovers what her father's penis is for. "It's a toothbrush!" she proudly announces to her mother. When the amused mother asks why she thinks that, the little girl explains that "this morning I saw the maid sliding it in and out of her mouth and she had toothpaste dripping down her chin".

Fieldwork

The fieldwork period stretched from 3 May 2003 to 22 August 2004 but with a number of breaks in order to spend some time with my family in England. My partner, the anthropologist Sarah Pink, and our toddler son, Vandon, accompanied me from October to January. My fieldwork base was a ninth-floor condominium flat located in the Subang Jaya precinct of USJ 6. From our living room windows we had a perfect view of the municipal council, located less than a ten-minute walk away (Figure 3.1). To the left of the council lay the commercial district known as Taipan, a triangle consisting mostly of shophouses, banks and restaurants with a multi-storey car park in the centre. To the right of the council were clearly visible the large detached houses of USJ 5 said to be occupied by wealthy residents. In the foreground, we could see row upon row of smaller terraced houses set along pleasant tree-lined streets. In front of the condo there was a neighbourhood green (*padang*) where every morning and evening local residents came to play basketball or badminton, exercise or socialise (Figure 3.2).

To reach Taipan from the condo on foot, we had to cross a busy road with no traffic lights or zebra crossings. This is a common feature in much of (sub)urban Malaysia where town planners have made scant allowance for pedestrians (Goh 2002). The assumption is that people will use their cars at all times. Not having a car made us into even more of an anomaly in Subang Jaya than being white, for it is only poor Malaysians and immigrant workers who are expected to have to rely on the substandard public transport. Once while waiting at a bus stop, a local woman took me for a liar when I told her that I had never owned a car and hardly ever drove in my own country. 'Everybody drives!', she

Figure 3.1. Subang Jaya's municipal council (MPSJ), a Malay-Muslim en-
clave in a Chinese-majority township.

countered, in what I translated as 'All but the poor drive, and you're
certainly not poor!'. When discussing the suburb's car-dependence with
local residents a common reply would go along these lines: 'We Malaysians don't walk. You see, it's too hot here'.

Having my own nuclear family for a period of time allowed me to
see and experience Subang Jaya from a very different perspective from
when I was on my own. For one thing, it gave me access to local families
that I would not have normally obtained or sought out. I also gained a
better, more empathetic insight into the difficulties faced by dual-career
families who struggle to reconcile the demands of work and family-
building. For example, reading about a past campaign for pedestrian
bridges following the death of a child who was run over by a car was not
only of research interest – it concerned us directly.

Sarah's expertise in visual anthropology, research methodology and
gender studies was helpful (see Pink and Murdock 2005). For example,
she soon noticed that most of my informants were male, and wondered
about women's participation in Internet activism and local governance.
In my defence, I should explain that this seeming gender bias was in
fact a result of the comparative research question that took me to Subang Jaya (agreed upon by a team of male and female anthropologists in
Europe). In classic ethnographic fashion, the two principles guiding my
fieldwork were: (a) 'Follow the action' and (b) 'If it matters to the locals,
then it matters to me'. Because my research question was what difference, if any, the Internet was making to residential governance, I had

Figure 3.2. The view from the author's fieldwork base, a condominium flat in the precinct of USJ 6. On the top left-hand corner is clearly visible the municipal council. To the right of the council lies the affluent neighbourhood of USJ 5. In the foreground, more affordable USJ 6 terraced houses and a local *padang*.

to spend time with individuals and groups who were actively involved in local issues, regardless of their age, gender, ethnicity, class or occupation. As said in Chapter 2, this was not a 'digital divide' study. As a result, many of my informants were not only men, but more specifically ethnic Chinese, middle-aged, middle-class men. I was not, after all, constructing a representative sample of Subang Jaya's vast population. Rather my objective was to identify and intensively research a single social universe (or field of practice) in an open-ended manner. Initially I used labels such as 'local e-Governance', 'local e-Communities', or 'community informatics' to refer to my object of study. It was only after fieldwork that I settled for the term I am using throughout the book, namely Subang Jaya's 'field of residential affairs'.[19]

The three main research methods I adopted were semi-structured interviews, participant observation (both online and offline) and archival research (mostly online). Semi-structured interviews such as the one that opens this chapter unfolded around a series of points that I wished to discuss but always in a dialogical, negotiated manner. Save for one or two interviewees who had no regular access to the Internet, I frequently followed up interviews via email. Another key method was participant observation in a wide variety of settings, particularly offline. Sites ranged from local greens, playgrounds and shops to the municipal council, pal council, street parties, official inaugurations, seminars, weddings, church services, and outreach campaigns. I also 'shadowed' some of my main informants as they went about their daily activities, paying particular attention to their Internet-related practices. In contrast, the online sites were less varied as the only busy site of online sociality was the Subang Jaya e-Community Portal (USJ.com.my). As I argue in Chapter 7, the portal's main forum is a thriving online environment in which 'thread sociality' predominates. This is a convivial, polylogical and asynchronous form of sociality with offline ramifications. My third main method was to visit the online (and a small number of offline) archives in order to research the history of local Internet activism and governance. Of special interest during fieldwork was the period between 1999 and 2004 – a well-recorded historical phase in which Subang Jaya's field of residential affairs became increasingly mediated by the Internet. After leaving Malaysia in August 2004 I pursued a second line of archival research aimed at reconstructing some of the main events that have taken place since my departure. The USJ.com.my archives were invaluable for both tasks (on geeks' 'archival hubris' and its methodological implications, see Kelty 2008).

The principal research language was Malaysia's middle-class lingua franca: English. For example, virtually all local Web forum posts in Subang Jaya are in this language. In some contexts I also used Malay, especially when interacting with taxi drivers and other low-income workers. Geographically, the bulk of research took place in Subang Jaya and especially in USJ where most of the Internet activity was concentrated. Additionally I attended a number of events and interviewed people in other parts of the Kuala Lumpur region, and made a short trip to the northern town of Ipoh to meet some of the local Internet 'champions' as well as to Penang to interview Subang Jaya's ex-municipal president, Datuk Ahmad Fuad.[20]

Notes

1. Interviewed in USJ on 16, 24 and 27 June 2004.
2. Sime UEP Annual Report (2003: 8).
3. Source: Patrick Tan, interviewed in USJ on 2 July 2004.
4. Ooi (1999), Sime UEP Annual Report (2003: 8).
5. Suthantiram (a member of the demolished temple committee), interviewed in USJ on 27 June 2004. See also www.usj.com.my/usjXpress/details.php3?table=usjXpress&ID=220
6. Aftar Singh, personal communication, 14 July 2004.
7. The first estimate is from Mohamad and Shahbuddin (2003), the second from

the municipal council.

8. From an undated PowerPoint presentation by Arpah Bt. Abdul Razak, Deputy President of Subang Jaya Municipal Council, entitled 'Improvement in public service through MPSJ's (Subang Jaya Municipal Council) experience'.

9. See http://asiarecipe.com/malgames.html

10. Malaysiakini, 10 October 2003, http://www.malaysiakini.com/news/20031010 00112531.php

11. See http://www.usj.com.my/bulletin/upload/printthread.php?t=23487

12. The study was conducted by MIRP Consult Sdn. Bhd, see http://www.hektar-group.com/SubangParade/Corporate/SP_Leasing_Brochure.pdf

13. Source: Arpah Bt. Abduk Razak, ibid. These figures may be unreliable, however. Thus according to the federal government's Yearbook of Statistics Malaysia (2007: 247) the total national average monthly expenditure per household was RM 1,631 in 1998/99 and RM 1,953 in 2004/05.
    http://www.statistics.gov.my/eng/index.php?option=com_content&view=article&id=401&Itemid=191

14. See http://biz.thestar.com.my/bizweek/story.asp?file=/2009/2/28/bizweek/33 55406&sec=bizweek

15. http://www.malaysiakini.com/letters/68670

16. http://www.washingtoncitypaper.com/articles/17711/welcome-to-chinaburb

17. http://www.usj.com.my/bulletin/upload/archive/index.php/t-26375.html

18. http://www.aliran.com/oldsite/monthly/2004b/10i.html

19. I should also note, in this context, that some of my key contacts in sites such as the residents' committees (JKP), the municipal council, the National IT Council and everyday locales in the suburb were indeed women.

20. Fuad went on to become mayor of Kuala Lumpur: http://thestar.com.my/metro/story.asp?file=/2009/8/24/central/4573973&sec=central

CHAPTER 4

Smarting Partners

In this chapter I start by telling the story of SJ2005, a top-down Internet project that sought to turn Subang Jaya into a 'smart community' by the year 2005. This local episode is part of the larger national story of governmental efforts to transform Malaysia into a technology-driven Knowledge Society by 2020. I then tell an overlapping story, only this time from a ground-up perspective: the story of how and why a local brand of Internet activism emerged in Subang Jaya in the late 1990s. This is an activism centred not on national or transnational affairs but rather on seemingly mundane local issues such as traffic congestion, waste disposal and crime prevention. I conclude with a brief survey of local Internet initiatives that lie just outside Subang Jaya's field of residential affairs and by addressing Wan Zawawi's crucial question (see Chapter 1) about those who are excluded from the field. By elucidating what the field is *not* we can begin to understand what kind of socio-technical universe the field actually is.

Federal Ambitions

One genealogical line of 'e-governance' efforts in Malaysia can be traced to the early 1990s when the Public Services Network (PSN) transformed the country's post offices into one-stop centres for service delivery. For the first time, outside agencies such as the Post Office or the investment holding company Permodalan Nasional Bhd (PNB) gained access to government-owned databases in order to reach businesses and citizens. This was as an early example of lowered barriers within the public sector and beyond (Karim and Khalid 2003: 16–17).

From the mid-1990s, the Malaysian government called for a move

towards a knowledge-based economy as the country faced growing com-
petition from Vietnam, China and other low-cost production econo-
mies. In 1996 a 'cyber-region' known as the Multimedia Super Corridor
(MSC) was carved out to the south of Kuala Lumpur. Designed as a
global centre for multimedia technologies and contents, its aim was to
'leapfrog' Malaysia from the Industrial Era to the Information Era. The
MSC was in line with Dr Mahathir's Vision 2020, the dream of a fully
developed, knowledge-driven Malaysia by 2020 (Yong 2003, cf. Nain
2004). One of the MSC's seven 'flagship applications' is e-Government.
Led by the Malaysian Administrative Modernisation and Management
Planning Unit (MAMPU), the aim of this flagship is to 'improve the
convenience, accessibility and quality of interactions with citizens and
businesses; simultaneously, it aims to improve information flows and
processes within government to enhance the speed and quality of policy
development, coordination and enforcement' (Yong 2003: 189). The
vision is 'for government, businesses and citizens to work together for
the benefit of the country and all its citizens' (2003: 190). Part of this
vision is the attainment of 'greater transparency' and accountability
(ITU 2002); in other words, better governance. Among the promised
technical innovations are the ability to settle utility bills and renew driving licences online through 'cashless transactions', initially in the Klang
Valley – the political and economic heartland of Malaysia where Subang
Jaya is located – but eventually across the country (Begum 2000).

While MAMPU's core business is the modernisation of Malaysia's
public sector, the government body directly concerned with local e-
Communities is the National IT Council (NITC), launched in 1996. The
NITC is a think tank that advises government on matters of ICT policy
and implementation. Its five key areas of activity are e-Community, e-
Public Services, e-Learning, e-Economy and e-Sovereignty (Nain 2004:
105). Progress, however, has been slow – as it has indeed been in most
other countries. E-government officials in Malaysia bemoan projects
that are often too large and unwieldy, a lack of inter-agency integration and common standards, a shortage of skilled workers, resistance
to change across the public sector, and other hurdles (Yong 2003: 196).
Scholars such as Nain (2004) have pointed out that Malaysia's e-Government initiatives suffer from ailments common to government projects
since independence in 1957. First and foremost, he singles out very low
levels of consultation with the citizenry. A more specific problem is that
in Malaysia's 'ethnocratic' regime (Leong 2008) Internet policies are
seldom linked to poverty eradication irrespective of race.

In 2002, the Malaysian Cabinet directed all local authorities 'to im-
plement e-Government services to benefit ratepayers'.[1] Local authori-

ties were encouraged to launch e-Community projects that would make them 'more accessible' to the residents.[2] That same year, the NITC's annual Infosoc Conference adopted the theme 'K-initiatives for Improved Local Governance'.[3] These eager calls arise from a troubled history. Over the decades, the Malaysian press has published countless letters of complaint against local authorities. Topics include over-development, traffic congestion, poor planning and maintenance of basic facilities, racial discrimination in the issuing of business licenses, corruption, and the absence of consultation with residents. NGO activists have linked the 'lack of ownership in governance processes' with episodic outbreaks of unrest and violence (Chandran 2003).

To activists who are lobbying for the reinstatement of local elections (but see Goh 2002), the fact that local councillors are appointed by the state government rather than elected makes them unresponsive to the ratepayers. Local elections were suspended by the Cabinet in 1965 when local councils in the hands of opposition parties made decisions independently from the Alliance federal government. A Royal Commission of Enquiry on Local Authorities was set up and its recommendations heard in 1968, including the maintenance of local elections despite their flaws. The government rejected this latter recommendation on the basis that the local authorities' key role in fostering urban development took precedence over their democratising role. It was imperative that local authorities should work in tandem with the federal and state governments for the sake of nation-building. As a result, today each political party within the ruling coalition (Barisan National or BN) is given a share of councillors' posts. Parties use this system to reward loyal individuals and factions. For this reason, it is not in the interest of the BN establishment, say the critics, to reintroduce local elections, as it would erode an old structure of patronage and political influence (Chandran 2003).[4]

Smarting Partners

SJ2005 was born in 1999, the brainchild of MIMOS, a corporatised government agency then in charge of Malaysia's ICT policy making. This was the year before the 'dotcom crash', a time when there was a strong faith across South East Asia in the imminent coming of the Information Age in tandem with democratic reform. Indeed *reformasi* was often seen as an almost inevitable by-product of the ICT revolution (Abbott 2004). SJ2005 was chaired by the then deputy prime minister, Abdullah Badawi who later became Malaysia's prime minister. It drew its inspiration both from Vision 2020 and from NITA, the National IT Agenda (John

2002). In addition to NITC and MIMOS, the partners were the Subang Jaya municipal council, the Ministry of Housing and Local Government (KPKT) and 'The Stakeholders', i.e., local residents and businesses. Although there was some talk of introducing participatory budgeting and local e-Elections, these 'democratic' ideas were soon rejected by the SJ2005 committee and partners.[5]

The first steering committee meeting was held in April 2000 (Ng 2002: 5). SJ2005's promoters envisioned transforming Subang Jaya into a 'smart', 'knowledge-based community' that would improve the residents' quality of life in a sustainable manner. Its objectives included increasing ICT awareness, easing Internet access, improving Internet and other ICT skills, creating a socially cohesive community, and evolving a 'good, effective, accountable, transparent, caring governance framework' (Ng 2002: 11). As the project manager Agnes Ng told me in an interview: 'We're not interested in small things like street lighting, we want to transform the community'.[6] The ambitious 2005 deliverables were:

- A high bandwidth telecommunication infrastructure that connects all users
- 100 per cent affordable household [sic] are connected and use Internet[7]
- An e-Community programme in each precinct
- Public services online
- A computing environment in all schools, educational institutions and where community learning is encouraged (formal and non-formal)
- Local business services over the Internet
- A Subang Jaya portal (www.sj2005.net.my) as a gateway to all e-Public Services, e-Business and e-Community products and services
- Impact evaluation of SJ2005 program[me] (Ng 2002: 12–13)

When talking to the SJ2005 pioneers about the early days, I was struck by a sense of great excitement. Participants from across the governmental divide truly believed that they could build a trisectoral partnership that would become a role-model for the rest of Malaysia.[8] We find an illustration of this shared hope in the USJ.com.my archives: a portrait showing a relaxed group of e-Community activists with a smiling Datuk Ahmad Fuad who was at the time the council president.[9]

Alas the excitement was short-lived, for SJ2005 was soon to run into serious difficulties.[10] One major bone of contention was the uneven allocation of federal funds. Both the municipal council and USJ.com.my had applied for funds from DAGS, a federal body entrusted with providing one-year seed funds for ICT projects. When neither organisation secured funding, they blamed the decision on MIMOS. In their defence, MIMOS countered that they were an entirely separate entity and that all

DAGS applications are subject to stringent, independent selection processes. It does appear, however, that MIMOS may have influenced the DAGS decision-making process, for instance by 'blacklisting' Jeff Ooi for his abrasive style and political independence.

Other factors contributing to the demise of SJ2005 may have included clashing personalities, rivalry over project ownership and recognition, and low levels of trust across organisations. One well-placed informant told me about a 'gap in expectations' between the various partners, in particular the municipal council, the state assemblyman and the 'communities' vis-à-vis their federal counterparts. This person also pointed at the low levels of funding, the limitations of volunteerism, an opaque authority structure, excessive politicking, institutional hurdles, and a lack of clear rewards. According to *Malaysian Business*:[11]

> 'Though mooted by NITC, other parties such as the MPSJ were keen to become owners of the project', says one source familiar with the project [probably Jeff Ooi, JP]. In the end, NITC held firm and kept a tight rein on the project. This injected the second dose of instability into the project's system. With these issues playing in the background, the SJ2005 committee, which consisted [of] three full time representatives from NITC, even had difficulty sourcing for office space within MPSJ's premise[s].

In addition to these factors, there was a deeper structural incompatibility at work between a top-down bureaucracy driven by targets and ground-up, open-ended initiatives such as USJ.com.my and Nwatch. In the current global parlance on governance, one of the mantras for the revival of local politics is the need for public participation and 'joining up government'. Following a comparative study of grassroots projects in Norway and Scotland, the anthropologists Abram and Cowell (2002: 1) have suggested that 'integration and participation are two … non-coherent principles that are merely presented together rather than analytically interwoven. As a result, producing holistic, comprehensive plans that involve direct participation of a broad range of community representatives presents innumerable, often insurmountable difficulties for authorities with large, diverse populations.'

Analogously, in the case of SJ2005 there was a clash between the two principles of integration and participation. On the one hand, a seamless integration of e-Government operations was presented as an unproblematic goal. In reality, when the municipal council (MPSJ) was created in 1997 it followed the practice of the day and allowed its various departments to purchase and run their own ICT applications according to their particular needs. Seven years later, under a new mayor, MPSJ hired a team of consultants to seek ways to integrate all applications onto a common platform – a process that will require long years of investment in labour, staff training and equipment.[12]

Participation was the other side of the SJ2005 coin. 'The community' was conceived of as a coherent entity potentially led by community 'champions'. These champions had to first 'buy into' a vision emanating from above, that is from NITC. It soon became clear, however, that 'the community' was as fractured and diverse as the various governmental partners recruited for SJ2005.[13]

To recapitulate, SJ2005 was a short-lived site of inter-sectoral contest rather than a platform for trisectoral integration and citizen participation, as envisaged by the federal internet policy makers.

Local Internet History

As we established in the previous chapter, Subang Jaya and its twin township, USJ, make up a largely middle-class, ethnic Chinese suburb of Kuala Lumpur. Most residents arrived in this award-winning suburb in the 1990s hoping to find a green and safe environment in which to raise their young nuclear families. Their plans were soon complicated, however, by a series of regional, national and local crises. In 1997 the collapse of South East Asia's financial markets caused a sharp economic downturn in Malaysia after many years of robust growth. A deep political crisis ensued when the then deputy prime minister, Anwar Ibrahim, was imprisoned without trial. This led to an explosion of pro-Anwar websites that Mahathir's government was unable to defuse, having guaranteed foreign investors that the Internet would remain free from governmental meddling.

It was precisely in 1997 that Subang Jaya's municipal council (MPSJ) was established. Two years later, in 1999, the new council faced the first in a long series of challenges from residents' groups when it raised local taxes by 240 per cent. The leading internet activist Jeff Ooi described the conflict in historic terms:

> We were furious. But before we could take up the matter with the council, we needed to gather and compile supporting evidence. Using the internet, we set up a residential database to compile data according to the type of houses, the assessment rates residents were paying, their contact numbers and so forth. Within two weeks, 50% of the community responded. The collective effort yielded a 20% reduction across the board. That was one of the milestones that proved how effective the internet was.[14]

This episode exemplifies the kind of 'banal activism' that has predominated in Subang Jaya and USJ ever since – an activism led by Internet-savvy residents who use the rhetoric of 'community' to campaign on issues such as taxation, traffic congestion, waste disposal, school provision and local crime (Chapter 1). These are issues that would seem mundane to the urban intelligentsia in Kuala Lumpur or to the young anti-globalisation activists in Barcelona studied by Juris (2008) but they are of crucial importance to suburban parents embarked on family-building projects (for other suburban examples, see Arnold et al. 2008, Durington 2007, Hampton 2003, Hampton and Wellman 2003, Mesch and Levanon 2003).

As a direct result of this local campaign, the Subang Jaya e-Community Portal (USJ.com.my) was founded by Jeff Ooi on 26 October 1999. The portal is a lively online environment that has continued to thrive to this day. It has two main areas: a 'community' forum and a local news site. At the time of writing (25 August 2009) the forum boasts 22,727 discussion threads, 344,634 posts and 30,754 registered members. Jeff had originally intended the forum to revolve around issues of local governance, but he finally accepted the majority view that 'small talk' should share pride of place with more weighty issues. As a result, local residents use the forum to discuss all manner of topics, from the pedestrian to the lofty, from local and national to world politics, from sports and travel to eating out. A hard core of enthusiasts even meet offline on a regular basis over a cup of *teh tarik*, a tea beverage popular in Peninsular Malaysia (Chapter 7).

The portal's news site (usjXpress) was another of Jeff's local innovations. In theory it is run by an editorial team of volunteers trained in 1999 by a local *Star* journalist, the late Harpajan Singh, but in actual practice it has always been Jeff's preserve. The investigative nature and critical – sometimes acerbic – tone of Jeff's editorials did not endear him to the municipal president, Ahmad Fuad (1997–2003), who often found himself on the receiving end of Jeff's sharp prose. In recognition of its influence with the municipal council, Steven Clift, an international authority on e-Democracy, singled out USJ.com.my as one of the world's very few 'city-wide online community discussion spaces with agenda-setting power' (quoted in Cashel 2003).[15]

Meanwhile, the municipal council continued to promote the SJ2005 ideal for some time despite having parted ways with their federal counterparts. A number of ambitious e-Community initiatives were launched by Arpah Bt. Abdul Razak, who was the deputy president of MPSJ until May 2005. These include a cyberschool, a cybermosque, three hypermedia libraries, three community ICT centres, a broadband network for middle- and low-income families, and a residents' committee portal (e-JKP). In 2003 the council was awarded two million ringgits from the Selangor state government towards ICT projects. One million was to be spent on new broadband facilities (both for e-Public Services and e-Community projects), and another million on initiatives aimed at bridging the so-called digital divide through more ICT centres.[16]

Worthy of special attention are the residents' committees (in Malay *Jawatankuasa Penduduk* or JKP) created by the council in 2001. These committees were set up in line with new community-orientated policies at Selangor State level, as well as being a response to USJ.com.my and other independent initiatives from the residents. Before leaving Subang Jaya to take up a high-profile post in Penang in August 2003, the municipal president, Ahmad Fuad, had left in charge of the JKP system the young man named Azli who we met during the seminar in Chapter 1. I had numerous conversations with Azli and followed him to the field a number of times. The epitome of Dr Mahathir's 'new Malay' (*Melayu baru*), Azli is an enterprising man eager to acquire new skills and to learn from others. He greatly enjoyed getting to know the residents and had an almost ethnographic appreciation of the importance of local knowledge. In spite of his relative youth and inexperience, he was respected by the residents as a rare local government servant who was committed to the community. One former JKP member found that Azli enjoyed 'getting involved' and had 'great potential'. However, as we might expect from his age and position, his dedicated *turun padang* ('going down to the ground') could not compensate for the mayor's (and deputy mayor's) prolonged absences from the field. As one JKP member put it to me: 'Azli is a nice guy but he doesn't make the decisions'. Another said: 'What's the point of setting up a JKP if things still don't get solved at the other end?'

When I first heard about the JKP system, I assumed it was either a public relations exercise or a novel form of indirect rule. Subsequent field research proved this first impression to be wrong. In actual practice, JKP members use the system to engage in complex two-way flows of information, consultation and influence with the local council. Although committee members – until 2008 all of them political appointees – are often frustrated with MPSJ's lack of action on issues ranging from clogged drains and traffic jams to burglaries, the system does provide residents with more clout than the older residents' associations (RAs).

The autonomy and potential of the JKP system was patently demonstrated in September 2004, when an alliance of residents' groups comprising USJ.com.my, Nwatch and the JKPs was formed to stop the building of a food court on land reserved for a police station (see Chapter 6). These groups were directly confronting the council who had discreetly approved the plan. Using a range of Internet and mobile technologies (such as private email, mailing lists, online forums, blogging, SMS) the residents swiftly mounted a demonstration that was covered by the mainstream press and several national television stations. This led to the intervention of the state government who halted the construction of the food court and eventually allocated funds for a police station under the 9th Malaysian Plan.

Nevertheless, the JKP system continues to develop and there are signs that it could be gradually moving towards greater democratisation. While previously all MPSJ councillors were political appointees, following the March 2008 general election 20 per cent of the new councillors are now drawn from the non-governmental sector. That is how Theresa Ratnam Thong, a JKP committee member whose work I knew well, came to be an MPSJ councillor. Whereas previously she could do little more than hope that the council would act on the concerns she raised on behalf of local residents, as the new chairwoman of Subang Jaya's Zone 1 she now has the mandate to make decisions and follow them through.[17] There are, however, local activists who remain sceptical. One of them told me over email that non-governmental councillors 'are no better than those devils in the old council'.

Unlike the JKP system as a whole, the e-JKP portal (jkpsj.org.my) has failed to make much progress. The contents are largely provided by MPSJ staff and few residents appear to make use of them. This can be partly attributed to local leaders' reluctance to open up a public discussion space in which they feel the terms would be set by the council rather than the residents.[18]

Let us consider now a third residential initiative with an Internet connection. In August 2001 Raymond Tan's USJ 18 Neighbourhood Watch scheme received federal funding under the umbrella of DAGS. The main aim of the generous seed grant of 1.124 million ringgits (c. 300,000 US dollars) was to enable Raymond and other volunteers to develop the Internet aspects of the scheme, including a professionally built web portal and ICT training for local residents. The sudden influx of substantial federal funds into a small corner of Subang Jaya's field of residential affairs sent shockwaves across the field. Two parties felt particularly aggrieved: the then municipal president, Ahmad Fuad, who protested that public monies were being lavished on a small neighbourhood project rather than on the local council, and Jeff Ooi who had hoped that his local portal, USJ.com.my, would be an integral part of SJ2005 but now felt it had been sidelined.

Although the funding of Nwatch strained relationships between Raymond Tan and Jeff Ooi, these improved in subsequent years. Their two 'e-Communities' are often seen as complementing each other, with Nwatch specialising in crime issues and USJ.com.my dealing with broader matters of local governance and quality of life. Indeed, several of USJ's more active residents regularly contribute to both initiatives. It is important to note, however, that USJ.com.my has always proudly declared its independence from government, whereas Nwatch has often worked closely with MPSJ, the police and the state assemblyman (Chapter 5).

This account of Subang Jaya's field of residential affairs would be incomplete without a brief reference to two key classes of local mediators: journalists and politicians. The online press, and in particular *The Star Online*, has arguably helped to strengthen local governance in Subang Jaya. Traditionally in Malaysia the press has allowed citizens a rare avenue for political expression on matters of local governance, which the ruling coalition deem less threatening than state- or federal-level matters (cf. Anttiroiko 2004). Although sceptics argue that this outlet is routinely abused by politicians to attack their rivals, it is also used by civic-minded residents through letters or emails to editors. The paradigmatic example of this latter contributor is Lau Bing, an elderly Subang Jaya resident and former JKP member who has published dozens of letters on local matters in the English-language press (Bing 2001). These letters on 'mundane' issues are in contrast to the more highbrow contributions on local governance by Citizen Nades and Goh Ban Lee regularly published by *The Sun*, a free newspaper that lacks an online version.

The Star has strong ties to Subang Jaya. With its head office in neighbouring Petaling Jaya, many of its journalists live in Subang Jaya. One of them, the late Harpajan Singh, was in fact involved in the foundation of USJ.com.my where he trained the editorial team.[19] Moreover, the various Internet groups in USJ frequently make use of contents from *The Star* directly relevant to their concerns. In some cases, published pieces have originated from the Internet activists themselves, e.g., an email to the editor on a local council action (or inaction).

In a country with declining standards of investigative journalism[20] and a government-controlled press (Gomez 2004), certain media can be counted on to publicise events favourable to government officials. Local politicians cannot take this for granted, though; they must cultivate good relations with journalists. The state assemblyman for Subang Jaya from 1995 to 2008, Dato' Lee Hwa Beng, who emerged from the middle-class grassroots, carefully cultivated such relations. During his thirteen-year tenure he was a regular fixture in the local press, both online and in print editions, in all three major languages (Chapter 5). Lee, an accountant with high ICT skills and a keen photographer, has had his own website (hwabeng.org.my) since 1995, the year he took office. On this website he would publish emails from residents and keep his constituents informed – albeit not always promptly – on matters affecting them. His role as a local governance go-between as well as his

Internet skills made him a respected figure across the Internet activism scene. In 2004 he was re-elected for a third consecutive term in office but in 2008 failed to secure a national parliamentary seat amidst a wave of discontent with the ruling coalition (of which his party, the Malaysian Chinese Association [MCA] is a key constituent member).

Beyond the Field

As discussed in Chapter 2, recent anthropological studies of the Internet have gone to great lengths to clarify what the Internet worlds under study are, as well as what they are not. Thus Kelty (2008) takes pains to explain that the transnational world of Free Software is a 'recursive public' and not an ordinary public sphere, nor is it an organisation, a collective, a crowd or a social movement. Similarly, Boellstorff (2008) explains that Second Life is definitely not a social networking site, a realm of 'virtual reality' or a sensational new world of consumerism and bizarre cybersex.

I will follow suit. Having just shown what makes the field of residential affairs 'a field' (and not a public sphere, a community or a network) I will now survey some of the Internet-related initiatives in Subang Jaya that lie just outside the field of residential affairs strictly defined, namely a campaign to bring back local elections, an NGO devoted to family matters, an organic food retailer, a failed blood bank and a youth football league. The reason I am placing them beyond the pale is that, in their own different ways, they all fail to engage with the municipal council's efforts to define and pursue residential governance goals. This is because their remit is either non-local or 'apolitical' (or both, in some cases), even when they are physically located in Subang Jaya.

Let us start with the forum on good local governance held in Subang Jaya's 3K Complex on 14 September 2003. This event brought to the suburb prominent figures from across Malaysia's pro-democracy movement active in a range of fields of practice, including human rights, journalism, social development, the law and academia, as well as leading residents and the then state assemblyman, Lee Hwa Beng. The stated aim of the forum was to discuss whether it was 'time to bring back local elections' to Malaysia after a hiatus of nearly 40 years (see above). Although a dedicated mailing list was set up and some efforts were made to take this issue forward after the event, the list has remained inactive. More importantly for our present purposes, this event had no noticeable effect on Subang Jaya's field of residential affairs. It may have been geographically located in the suburb, with some hopes being raised that local Internet activists may take their activism 'to the next level', but this initiative failed to capture the local activist imagination.[21]

In marked contrast, Family Place (familyplace.com.my) whose motto is 'Bridging Families, Building Communities' is an undoubted Subang Jaya success story. This website and yahoogroup was founded by KV Soon – a USJ.com.my pioneer – and his wife, Chong Wai Leng.[22] KV had previously been involved in a number of IT start-ups, 'from zero up to 50 million US'. They started in 1997 with a website on baby and toddler care. In those days websites were not popular, and most of their contents spread by word of mouse. Chong and Soon also organised regular face-to-face gatherings on parenting. As their children and those of other network participants grew older, priorities shifted 'from babies and diapers to education'. Among Chinese parents one main area of concern is whether or not to send their children to Mandarin-medium schools. Although most Family Place parents are English-educated, many now feel a Mandarin education is important. Another option is home schooling, which Soon and Chong themselves practise, as do a number of parents within the network. They find that the Malaysian school system does not provide adequate educational or emotional development. To them, Malaysian kindergartens are replicas of primary schools. 'They're very stressful, something's not right.' There should be, in their view, more play and less writing.[23] Yet Family Place, they insist, does not advocate home schooling for all: 'We advocate a more democratised system, more choices for education'.

In 1999 Family Place was the recipient of DAGS funding. 'It allowed us to go public, as there was a fantastic amount of publicity.' With the new funds, they could afford to hire website specialists, researchers, writers and even a PR consultant. They also attended SJ2005 working committee meetings on e-Community but found them top-down and not sufficiently community-minded. Today Family Place sustains itself through a range of educational programmes for parents and children[24] and it has continued to innovate technologically, with a podcast feature introduced in June 2007. It has also acquired a more overtly militant tone, albeit on national rather than local issues, such as campaigning against Malaysia's National Service following reports of the deaths of up to twenty young recruits.[25]

Two members of the Family Place network are Adelyn and Calwinn, who run an organic retail company named Good4u (good4u.com.my). Although they have a website and receive email orders daily, the one indispensable technology in their business is the mobile phone. From their USJ home and Calwinn's mother's in Petaling Jaya, they serve the entire Klang Valley. Adelyn used to run an accountancy software firm. Calwinn sold audiovisual equipment, but after the late 1990s recession collecting money 'became terrible'. 'We didn't get to see much of the family. After the crisis we did a lot of rethinking.' They wanted to raise a healthy family but felt new hypermarkets such as Giant were not up to their standards. Searching for alternatives, they found a free-range chicken supplier in the Bentong area: 'A bit pricey but we were happy. Then we thought, "Why don't we distribute the chicken?", as we had been passing it onto friends and family already. Chicken is very common, everybody eats it. We were searching for wholesome food.'

Since they had committed themselves to home schooling, their new business had to be compatible with it. They use their home to process orders and Calwinn's mother's as the distribution centre, with stocks kept in both. When my family became their customers in November 2003, they had a 'slow' website in the process of being upgraded to keep up with a growing customer base. The web-based software was developed by a friend. In the evenings they would compile databases to analyse the buying trends. Nearly six years on, as I write these lines in August 2009, they are still in business and offer a broader range of products via their much upgraded site.

Another 'e-Community' initiative, in this case unsuccessful, was the Blood Donors' List.[26] Started by Satish Janardanan,[27] jocosely known as Mr Dracula, it achieved a list of seventy names but has remained inactive since mid-2002. Satish, who is of North Indian descent, belongs to the regionally rare 'O-negative' blood group, shared by only twelve thousand people in Malaysia.[28] Given the lack of public cooperation, the list died 'a natural death', Satish told me.

Unlike the Blood Bank, the Subang Jaya Community Youth Football League is very much alive and kicking. The league was started in 2000 by an American resident of USJ, Douglas Ladner, in collaboration with a multiethnic group of Malaysians.[29] The driving principle, imported from the United States, is captured in the motto "A league for kids where everyone plays and no one is paid". 'As the motto suggests, the heart of the league is a spirit of volunteerism in the pursuit of positive family values. Football is not simply an end in itself, but a means to much higher social and personal goals' (Douglas Ladner, 4 August 2004 email).

This core vision has been carefully adapted to Malaysia's official ideology, with a stress on family, community service and interracial harmony. As a basic rule, at least one parent must become involved in coaching and supporting their children. Indeed some single parents have joined the League. Judging by a field visit in February 2004, the various ethnic groups are well represented, not a mean achievement in a country where sporting preferences are closely bound up with ethnicity (see Chapter 2). The League does however seem to be largely a middle-class affair. For instance, during fieldwork League members carried out a charity drive resulting in the donation of food hampers to poor families.[30]

The League covers the entire MPSJ area but some families from other areas also take part, having learned about it through its well-designed website (sjcyfl.com). The website has a handful of dedicated content producers, and the League is also supported by a regular mailing list. The volunteers who man the organisation hope it will become a model to be replicated across the country.[31] The Ministry of Sport has already indicated its friendly wish to 'hijack' the League, although the League has so far remained resolutely independent. While welcoming the MPSJ logo and logistical support, the League is fully self-governing. League members describe it as a 'close-knit community' where one befriends people who would otherwise remain suburban strangers. To foster this process of community-building, parties, outings and other social events are regularly held.

The Excluded

I have just reviewed some of the new connections amongst Subang Jaya residents enabled or enhanced by the Internet, including residents' forums, community journalism, Neighbourhood Watch schemes, parental groups, and a politician's website. Yet we should bear in mind that this 'imperative to connect' (Green, Harvey and Knox 2005) frequently results in disconnections as well as connections (Appadurai 1986, Strathern 1996). It is important, then, to ask, as did Wan Zawawi in the seminar that opens Chapter 1: Who are the people being connected and disconnected by these various Internet initiatives? Are there any significant ethnic, religious, class, gender, or age divides at work?

First, let us consider the 'well-connected' in Subang Jaya. The profiles of e-community founders and active members show interesting commonalities. Most innovators were at the time of fieldwork (2003-2004) in their 40s and combined internet expertise with social and political acumen. Most of them lived in USJ and were ethnic Chinese, English-educated and employed or self-employed in the private sector. They moved into USJ in the 1990s with young families and middle-class expectations of a good quality of life in a premier township. Yet instead of realising the Malaysian dream, they encountered clogged roads and drains, dwindling green spaces, alarming crime statistics and declining educational standards. Having lived through – and often led – Internet innovations in the private sector, they found a municipal council (MPSJ) that was struggling to keep abreast of social and technological changes and seemed unprepared to engage with the residents.

Subang Jaya's 'e-Community' experiments range from the highly active to the inactive, from the official to the independent, from the Internet-based to the Internet-related. In at least one case, the lines between 'e-Community' and 'e-Business' are blurred – witness the overlap between Family Place and Good4u in their 'wholesome', family-centred values and aspirations. They all have in common an early engagement with issues directly affecting the welfare and prospects of their own families, such as taxation, traffic, crime, parenting, education, and health. From that direct experience in an underserviced suburbia, and except for the now defunct Blood Bank, these initiatives grew by word of mouse, supported by mailing lists, websites, portals and mobile phones. It follows from this collective profile that many non-Chinese, elderly, young, foreign, and low-income residents are being 'disconnected' from these creative forms of internet appropriation. The exact mechanisms at work in these systemic exclusions are, however, beyond the scope of this study.

Notes

1. Victoria Government (2002a).
2. Victoria Government (2002b).
3. Infosoc Malaysia (2002).
4. The former prime minister, Dr Mahathir bin Mohamad, has defended the appointment of councillors as a way of avoiding electoral campaigns 'dominated by politics' (Bernama 2003). Critics counter, nonetheless, that the system lacks transparency. For example, local authorities, including MPSJ, are said to be misusing the Official Secrets Act to hoard information from the public. Additionally, 'non-compliance' with local government rules is rife. Observers often point out, however, that it is not only residents who flout the bylaws. Owing to 'excessive regulations, ineffective laws and the laxity in meting out punishment against corrupt officials' (Teophilus 2002), non-compliance is reportedly practised by citizens, civil servants and politicians alike (Goh 2002). In 2003, Mahathir blamed the local councillors' laxity on their desire to remain popular. In such cases, he added, the federal government would have to 'force them' (Bernama 2003). Around that time, his then deputy, Abdullah Badawi, chaired a Cabinet Committee on Good Governance to discuss issues of local government enforcement and efficiency (Ooi 2003). Upon becoming prime minister in October 2003, Badawi insisted on the critical importance of 'frontline' services, especially those at the local government level, but little actual change on the ground came of these entreaties.
5. See www.malvu.org for a reaction to this paper that stresses the lack of democratic freedoms in Malaysia in comparison with Thailand, Indonesia or the Philippines.
6. Interviewed at MIMOS Bhd, 25 Jun 2004.

7. In grammatically correct English: 'All households that can afford it will be connected to, and use, the Internet'. The 'affordable' qualifier was not in the original formulation of the deliverables.

8. The trisectoral idea was borrowed from Local Agenda 21 (LA21), derived from the UN Conference on Environment and Development (UNCED) held in Rio de Janeiro in 1992 (Chandran 2003).

9. See http://www.usj.com.my/aboutus.php3.

10. Strictly speaking, and from a MIMOS/Sigma perspective, SJ2005 is still alive through an e-business project (e-BizX) as well as an initiative aimed at modernising the local shoe industry by means of new ICTs. These initiatives are being pursued independently from MPSJ.

11. S. Jai Shankar, 'Whatever happened to SJ2005?' Malaysian Business, 1 September 2005, http://findarticles.com/p/articles/mi_qn6207/is_20050901/ai_n24909 318/?tag=content;col1.

12. MPSJ is not alone in the lack of interoperability of its applications. Over the last three decades, the Malaysian government has invested more than RM 3 billion on computerisation. Yet the result has been 'pockets of automation' lacking common standards that would allow information and system sharing across agencies (Karim and Khalid 2003: 36–37). The pace of overall change was so uneven that the federal government allowed each agency and department to adopt ICTs at their own pace. Today the government is questioning the wisdom of such a strategy and has created the Government Integrated Telecommunications Network (GITN). Officials have frequently reported a resistance to integration throughout the Malaysian public sector (2003: 81–87) – as have indeed researchers working on e-government projects in Europe (Kubicek et al. 2003).

13. On the conceptual difficulties and controversies that surround the notion of 'community', see Rapport (1996), Amit (2002) and Amit and Rapport (2002).

14. http://thestar.com.my/special/online/usjweb/default.htm#Mobilizing%20 networks.

15. See http://dowire.org/wiki/Community_Forums_and_News_in_Subang_J.

16. Arpah Bt. Abdul Razak, interviewed at MPSJ on 20 May and 6 December 2003. Reportedly the most successful initiative to date has been the hypermedia library, but I have yet to analyse in detail these varied projects.

17. http://thestar.com.my/metro/story.asp?file=/2008/7/25/central/21904651& sec=central.

18. In contrast, Ipoh City Council (MBI), in the northern Peninsular state of Perak, hosts a community forum which had yielded a modest, yet significant, output of 118 topics and some 600 posts, both in English and Malay, as of 14 July 2004 (see www.forum.mbi.gov.my). Some of these posts are critical of the local authorities, yet there would seem to be neither censorship nor any other form of moderation. This has made participants feel that they are 'talking to the wall'.

19. See www.usj.com.my/harpsgdn/harpsgdn.php3.

20. R. Nadeswaran alias Citizen Nades (*The Sun*), interviewed in Petaling Jaya on 1 July 2004.

21. The issue has recently resurfaced, however. Thus a Subang Jaya debate on whether local council elections should be restored in Malaysia was chaired by the state assemblywoman, Hannah Yeoh, on 7 June 2009. See http:// edwardling.blogspot.com/2009/06/should-local-council-elections-be.html.

22. Interviewed in Subang Jaya (USJ) on 18 October 2003.

23. According to the Australian psychologist Michael Carr-Gregg, Malaysian pupils spend an average of 3.8 hours a day on homework. In contrast, the figure is 3.5 for Singapore, 2.2 for Canada, 2.1 for the US, 2 for Australia and New Zealand, and 1.7 for Japan (Almeida 2004).

24. See www.unescobkk.org/education/ict/v2/detail.asp?id=1349.

25. See http://familyplace.tmspublisher.com/article.cfm?id=284.

26. http://yahoo.com/group/usj_subangjaya.

27. Telephone interview on 22 October 2003. Email communication on 10 August 2004. See also http://www.usj.com.my/usjXpress/details.php3?table=usjXpress&ID=112. Satish plans to move the Blood List database to a new message board: http://groups.yahoo.com/group/ usjCommunity.

28. http://www.usj.com.my/usjXpress/details.php3?table=usjXpress&ID=112.

29. Interviewed in Subang Jaya (USJ) on 10 February 2004.

30. Further research would be required to settle this matter, however. According to their website, 'One of the strengths of the club is the diversity it represents. In addition to the obvious ethnic diversity and deliberately balanced teams, our players and more than 200 families members reflect tremendous socio-economic differences. Volunteer coaches and team managers have been parents and kind souls representing all walks of life'. http://sjcyfl.wetpaint.com/page/Who+We+Are.

31. The model has already been adopted in neighbouring Bukit Jelutong, Shah Alam (see www.asianewsnet.net/level3_template1.php?l3sec=6&news_id=26873).

CHAPTER 5

Personal Media

The proliferation of personal media (for example, email, homepages, personal blogs, online profiles, mobile phones, iPods and iPads) has attracted a great deal of journalistic and scholarly interest, most recently in connection to Barack Obama's reported fondness for his BlackBerry.[1] A number of scholars have linked the diffusion of personal media to the rise of the Network Society, and more specifically to the rise of 'networked individualism' (Chapter 2) – the claim that social relationships are being reconfigured away from the place-based collectives that were dominant in previous eras (families, communities, associations) and towards a new pattern of sociality built around increasingly autonomous individuals (Castells 2001, Wellman 2001, 2002, Wellman et al. 2003, Wesch 2008). The influential social theorist Manuel Castells writes:

> From very different perspectives, social scientists, such as Giddens, Putnam, Wellman, Beck, Carnoy, and myself, have emphasized the emergence of a new system of social relationships centered on the individual. After the transition from the predominance of primary relationships (embodied in families and communities) to secondary relationships (embodied in associations), the new, dominant pattern seems to be built on what could be called tertiary relationships, or what Wellman calls "personalized communities", embodied in me-centered networks. It represents the privatization of sociability … The new pattern of sociability in our societies is characterized by networked individualism (Castells 2001: 128–29).

For Wellman (2002) personal media such as mobile phones allow individuals to communicate directly with other individuals regardless of location, thereby overcoming the constraints of earlier forms of place-to-place communication, namely landlines. These technologies contribute to the rise of networked individualism through their 'personalisation, wireless portability and ubiquitous connectivity' (Wellman et al. 2003: 16; see also Castells et al. 2007). Mobile phones, adds Cameron (2006), have evolved rapidly from being mere telephony devices to becoming 'portable, personal media hub[s]' that enable a growing range of 'personalised and customised communication, entertainment, relationship management and service functions'. More dramatically, Saffo (2007) claims that we are in the midst of a personal media 'revolution' analogous to the TV-centric mass media revolution of the 1950s. If watching television was a living room practice in which families consumed the products of a few major 'players', personal media practices are carried out everywhere by countless small players creating their own contents.

Other scholars, many of them anthropologists, are sceptical of these claims that new media technologies herald the advent of a global era of networked individualism (e.g., Agar et al. 2002, Amit 2007, Green et al. 2005, Hogan 2009, Horst 2008, Horst and Miller 2006, Knox et al. 2006, Riles 2000). Thus the communication scholar Marika Lüders (2008: 696), whilst conceding that the widespread adoption of personal media is bound to have important social and political consequences, argues that it is 'naïve' to seek to 'identify any profound transformative message of personal media'. On the basis of empirical research in Norway she rejects any sharp distinction between personal and mass media. For example, Norwegians use email not only for interpersonal but also for mass communication, e.g., emailed newsletters. Moreover, adds Lüders, collaborative and group media such as collective blogs or wikis are neither strictly personal nor mass media (2008: 698–99). Personal media can only be understood, therefore, as part of an increasingly complex and shifting communicative landscape. Laying a similar stress on complexity, the anthropologists Heather Horst and Daniel Miller follow Harper (2003) in rejecting the 'fairly unreconstructed Durkheimian lament' about the loss of 'social capital' that networked individualism theorists claim accompanies the reported rise of egocentric networking. Following ethnographic research on mobile phones in Jamaica, these authors call for more cross-cultural research that will show 'how much more subtle the relationship between individuals and wider networks can be today and how much more complex their relationship has been in the past' (Horst and Miller 2006: 81; see also Downey 2008, Horst 2008).

Along similar lines, Vered Amit (2007; and this volume, Chapter 1) encourages anthropologists not to jump on the network society 'bandwagon' but to reclaim instead the original Manchester School promise of the notion of network as a device that allows researchers to follow individuals across enduring sets of social relations – groups, associations, organisations (see also Knox et al. 2006). Amit undertook research among Montreal-based consultants who frequently travel to developing countries. Borrowing Granovetter's (1973) classic principle of 'the strength of weak ties' (the notion that friends of friends are more useful than close friends or family for certain goals such as finding a job or a partner), she argues that these professionals' occupational networks are shaped through the dispersal of reputations and 'episodic mobilisation of instrumental and frequently transient relationships', i.e., through the mobilisation of weak ties (Amit 2007: 57). This author advocates an exploratory approach to networks that will not peg them to any particular methodology (Hannerz 1980) or a priori categories (e.g., 'diaspora'), but stressing that conceptual clarity is essential (Amit 2002). For example, we should not conflate the notions of 'personal network' and 'social group':

> Personal networks are not simply the means for the creation of organized communities. Such networks operate in their own right and on distinctive terms. They are ego-based, that is to say they arise through particular individuals' efforts, experiences and history ... This ... is a framework of social linkage that requires perhaps the most intensive, self-conscious and constant efforts from its key protagonists, but which is also the most structurally ephemeral.
>
> This is a very different form of organization than more enduring social groups whose basis for mobilization is institutional or communal. Such groups do not rely for their rationale or configuration on any one individual. They can thus survive, to a greater or lesser degree, shifts in personnel (Amit 2002: 22–23).

In this chapter I join the ongoing anthropological rethinking of networks that is taking place under conditions of swift technological change around the globe. I do so through case studies of the personal media practices of three Subang Jaya leaders: Lee Hwa Beng, Jeff Ooi and Raymond Tan. Like the other anthropologists just mentioned, I am sceptical of claims that we are moving towards a new global order built around the ego-centred networks and personal media of individuals. If anything, the available evidence suggests that personal media are contributing, together with other media, to the ongoing diversification of 'sociocentric' formations around the globe (online game worlds, peer groups, youth gangs, political cliques, professional fields, fan clubs, urban subcultures, activist networks, and so on) – not to the replacement of one single 'dominant pattern of sociability' by another (Castells 2001: 128–29). This is certainly the case in Subang Jaya, a suburb where personal media have coexisted with, and co-shaped, a myriad of sociocentric formations since the early 1990s. Building on field concepts from Bourdieu (1993, 1996) and the Manchester School of Anthropology

(Epstein 1958, Evens and Handelman 2006, Postill 2007, Turner 1974), I track the public trajectories and personal media practices of three local leaders as they operate across a number of social fields. This hybrid field/network analysis (cf. Nooy 2003, Moeran 2002, 2005) shows that local leaders' personal media are often put to collectivist not individualist uses. It also supports Lüders's contention (2008 and above) that personal media cannot be considered in isolation from either collective media or mass media. Far from promoting egocentrism in the suburb, personal media have been central to the emergence of a staunchly communitarian field of residential affairs in which exhibiting the strength of one's weak ties in public is actively discouraged.

The second aim of this chapter is more empirical: to add to the ethnographic record on digital media and local-level leadership, a question about which we still know very little (Coleman 2005). This is an area of research ripe for collaboration between two anthropological subfields that have yet to acknowledge their mutual existence, namely political anthropology and media anthropology. Anthropologists have long been fascinated by the varied media entanglements of charismatic leaders, indigenous activists and social entrepreneurs.[2] However, most existing studies were undertaken before the proliferation of personal media and have not engaged with the debate around networked individualism that occupies us here.

I turn now to the personal media practices of three Subang Jaya leaders, all three early adopters of technological innovations (see Rogers 1995). The first is the elected politician Lee Hwa Beng who uses his personal website, email, digital cameras and other personal media to document his indefatigable service to local residents in tandem with the pro-government press. The second is the often mentioned Jeff Ooi who started as a local Internet activist but went on to achieve renown as a political blogger, international speaker and Member of Parliament, and yet must still abide by the law of selfless volunteerism when operating within Subang Jaya's field of residential affairs. Finally, the third profiled leader is Raymond Tan, a Neighbourhood Watch activist whose personal media practices are again shaped by the field's communitarian ethos, as seen by his efforts to disassociate his business activities from his 'community' work.

From a field-theoretical perspective, these local leaders are best described as 'leading practitioners' within the field of residential affairs. This means that they need to demonstrate their skilled embodied abilities both in the field's 'stations' (Giddens 1984) – the 'stopping places' where field agents interact on a regular basis – and in the field's more volatile and irregular 'arenas', those field sites in which political actors are obliged to state publicly and unambiguously where they stand on an unresolved dispute (Turner 1974). In the present era both stations and arenas are becoming increasingly mediated through digital technologies, including personal media such as email, blogs, and mobile phones. In the technophiliac and collectivist world of Subang Jaya's residential affairs, a leader who makes public use of the latest personal media will be well regarded, but only if they can demonstrate that they are using their 'digital personalia' (cf. Gell 1986) to serve the common good.

Proof of the padang

Lee Hwa Beng was born in 1954 and raised on an estate near Malacca where his father worked as a rubber tapper. Money was scarce and Lee had to cycle to school because his family could not afford the forty sen bus fare. Yet he persevered with his studies and eventually earned professional qualifications as an accountant, setting up his own accounting firm in Kelana Jaya, a district that borders Subang Jaya.[3] Lee rose to local notoriety in the 1990s for leading a vigorous campaign to rid Subang Jaya of rats – a campaign that earned him the friendly soubriquet of 'Ratman'. In 1995 he was elected state assemblyman for Subang Jaya with MCA, the ethnic Chinese component of Barisan Nasional (BN), the country's ruling coalition since independence in 1957. An affable person with a reputation for being hardworking and dedicated to his constituents, he was re-elected in 1999 and 2004 but lost his seat in 2008 when he stood for Parliament but failed to be elected. His state assembly post went to a young female opposition candidate amidst a nationwide wave of discontent with BN that saw the ruling coalition lose its two-thirds majority and control of five state assemblies (Singh 2009).

Personal media technologies have been integral to Lee's political practice from the outset. As noted in the Photo-Essay, he launched his own personal website as early as 1995 so as to 'further enhance my service to the community', adding that this was 'a revolutionary step' to take for a Malaysian politician. Throughout his thirteen-year tenure (from 1995 to 2008) Lee used his website to reach out to his constituents, sometimes at the cost of public criticism. Thus, in January 2002 he posted an email from a resident who chided him for not delivering on his promise of a Chinese school for Subang Jaya. Thanking his constituent for his 'kind words', Lee explained that far from having been idle, he had in fact held lengthy meetings with high-ranking officials and politicians.

> Therefore, everything is under control. It is better for me to show action than talk. Residents like you will judge me by my actions and deeds and not by my words. Thanks again.

Figure 5.1. The proof of the *padang*. The author with the then state assemblyman for Subang Jaya, Lee Hwa Beng, 16 November 2003. He is holding a photograph that Lee has just printed of the two of them with his mini photo printer (a personal medium) during a youth basketball tournament launched by Lee to foster better ethnic relations in the suburb.

Yours In Service,

Lee Hwa Beng
ADUN[4] Subang Jaya

Lee made this very point again during a fundraising dinner organised by the USJ Residents' Association that I attended in December 2003 (see Photo-Essay), but adding on this occasion a reference to residents' own duties. Having thanked his hosts for a splendid meal, he then exhorted the audience to join his newly formed volunteer police force. The message was clear: the proof of the *padang* is not in the eating but in the doing.

Another personal medium recruited to Lee's political groundwork was the digital camera. During his tenure Lee regularly used digital photography to document and publicise his local troubleshooting. For example, in October 2003 he inaugurated a guardhouse in a small residential area of USJ. He spoke glowingly in Malay and English about the residents' hard work over the previous three to four years. The results, both physical (the guardhouse) and non-physical (a strong community spirit)[5] were plain for all to see – and for all to photograph, he may have added. He then proceeded to ceremonially cut the ribbon and to pose for the press cameras in front of the guardhouse, after which he was interviewed by a young reporter locally regarded as an MCA mouthpiece 'who always follows him around'. The mediated practice of documenting Lee's groundwork was not restricted, though, to friendly press photographers and reporters. At other times it also involved his aides, local residents and even this anthropologist. On at least one occasion he presented a resident with an expensive digital camera which came, as the resident put it, 'with strings attached' for it was to be used to photograph Lee as he went about solving local issues. An ostensibly 'personal' medium was being recruited into a traditional patron–client arrangement (see Gomez and Jomo 1997).

In all of these cases, Lee was exploiting the specific affordances of photography to serve the *turun padang* imperative, notably its indexicality, that is, the direct physical bond that links a photographic image with its object (Knappett 2002). With these photographs, and across a range of media supports, Lee was providing documentary evidence not only of his constant 'being there' (Geertz 1988) but also of working towards solving local problems.

From Cyberactivist to MP

I turn now to the personal media practices of a leading USJ resident, Jeff Ooi. At first sight Jeff Ooi's life trajectory bears a strong resemblance to that of Lee Hwa Beng. Like Lee, Jeff was born in the mid-1950s and raised in a provincial ethnic Chinese household of modest means (his father was a lorry driver in the northern Malaysian state of Kedah). Similarly, despite these humble beginnings, Jeff too managed to attain professional qualifications and a private-sector career whilst becoming a local leader in Subang Jaya and USJ. In Jeff's case, the qualification was an MBA in international management that led to a career as an ICT consultant for a transnational advertising firm.

Although both are personal trajectories of social mobility and migration typical of the 'new middle classes' around the developing world,[6] on closer inspection there are notable differences as well. Whilst Lee is generally regarded as an affable mediator and peacemaker, Jeff is renowned for his confrontational style. Moreover, as an MCA politician Lee has always represented the political establishment, whereas Jeff's public persona is that of a proudly independent community activist and blogger who in 2008 became a Member of Parliament (MP) with the opposition's Democratic Action Party (DAP).[7] Despite being only two years Lee's junior, in the oppositional imaginary Jeff belongs to a new 'Internet generation' of young ented Malaysians whose mission is to lead the nation towards a democratic Knowledge Society and away from the ruling coalition's bankrupt racial politics – a persona that Jeff himself has assiduously cultivated.[8]

Jeff first caught the public eye in Subang Jaya and USJ in 1999 as a leading figure in the earlier mentioned campaign against a steep rise in local taxes. Following the success of this mobilisation, and having failed to set up a local e-Business venture in the harsh post-1997 economic climate, he turned to local e-Community building. This newfound interest materialised in the Subang Jaya e-Community Portal (USJ.com.my), described in Chapter 4. When I first met Jeff in May 2003 (Chapter 3) he had just found a more prominent platform for his citizen journalism: political blogging on national rather than local issues. Four months earlier, in January 2003, he had launched the blog 'Screenshots' under the motto "Thinking Aloud, Thinking Allowed". Screenshots swiftly rose to national acclaim in reformist circles for its bold denouncing of poor governance and corruption in Malaysia's corridors of corporate and governmental power. Locally, however, fellow activists were concerned that Jeff's blogging would take time away from his grassroots work in the suburb. These fears were to prove well founded in subsequent years.

One key to the success of Screenshots was Jeff's growing network of sources across a range of powerful fields – journalists, lawyers, politicians, Internet activists, CEOs. These 'little birds', as Jeff calls them, leak him information on the foul play of the powerful that mainstream news media will not publish. Often the mainstream media themselves have come under Jeff's scrutiny. For instance, in June 2004 a *New Straits Times* editor emailed Jeff to advise him that their editor-in-chief had blocked access to Screenshots from their premises. Jeff duly published extracts from this email taking care to protect the identity of his little bird, thus embarrassing the senior journalist in question.

Jeff's blogging freedom was severely tried in October 2004 when an anonymous Screenshots poster made some remarks that were deemed by senior government and media figures to be insulting to Islam. Jeff was questioned by the police and there were concerns in pro-democracy circles that he could be arrested without trial under Malaysia's draconian Internal Security Act (ISA). His case was taken up by the Paris-based organisation Reporters Without Borders who in 2005 gave Screenshots the Freedom Blog Award for Asia. With this international backing in place, Jeff continued to blog about highly sensitive issues, such as the April 2006 conflict that pitted Malaysia against Singapore over the causeway connecting the two countries (George 2007).

Jeff still reports on Subang Jaya via the USJ.com.my portal (see food court campaign below) but these interventions are now few and far between owing to his many other commitments. These include frequent engagements as an invited speaker on new media and citizen journalism at prestigious venues such as Reuters in London, the World Summit of the Information Society in Tunisia, and the Harvard Law School in Massachusetts.[9] The marked contrast in how news of his Harvard invitation was received in the fields of political blogging and residential affairs is instructive. Thus an admirer and fellow Malaysian blogger reported that at Harvard Jeff had 'networked with some of the world's leading bloggers'. He then quoted Jeff approvingly: "'I do these international talks to cover my ass," he says. "If I ever get detained or arrested, I know it'll be on CNN"'.[10] However, when Jeff mentioned his Harvard invitation on his own USJ.com.my forum he provoked the following reaction: 'usj.com.my is a community website (unless i am wrong). It is NOT a primary site as intellectual forum for show offs, wannabes and what nots ... I do not give a flying banana about mit, oxford or harvard talk. I have that already in the office and in any half decent pubs.'

What are we to make of these diametrically opposed reactions to the same news? Is the second reaction merely an outburst of 'flaming' from an irate individual who is breaching the forum's netiquette? This would be an unsatisfactory explanation. From a field-theoretical perspective, what is interesting about these contrasting reactions to Jeff's Harvard talk is what they reveal about the contrasting logics of two different fields of practice – logics that social leaders ignore at their own peril. In Malaysia's emergent field of political blogging, showing off one's 'strength of weak ties' (Granovetter 1973), i.e., a robust personal portfolio of connections, is not only acceptable, in fact it is seen as offering some measure of protection against an authoritarian government averse to negative publicity. By contrast, such bragging is anathema in Subang Jaya's field of residential affairs where, as said earlier, a staunch egalitarianism pervades the public discourse.

In early 2007 Jeff was courted by the opposition's Democratic Action Party (DAP) and finally joined their ranks in June. Contesting in the 2008 general elections as a DAP candidate for a seat in Jelutong, in the northern state of Penang, he won by a majority margin and became a Member of Parliament.[11] He was also DAP's national e-campaign director in the run-up to the elections. Although he did not blog frequently during the campaign, it is safe to assume that his reputation as Malaysia's top political blogger contributed to this electoral success.[12]

I turn now to the third and final profile, that of Raymond Tan, a USJ Neighbourhood Watch activist whose personal media practices are as shaped by the collectivist logic of the field of residential affairs as those of Lee Hwa Beng and Jeff Ooi.

The Crimewatcher

Raymond Tan was born in 1960, the fourth of ten siblings and the only one to be schooled in English rather than Mandarin, a language that he hopes to learn on retiring so as to study his own faith, Taoism. With an engineering background, he worked in the oil and gas industry for fifteen years. 'Sick and tired' of political intrigues in the corporate world, he left the industry in 2002. In recent years he has become involved in multilevel marketing, a line of business that he regards as 'a perfect platform to gain control of my own time if I am to be able to continuously participate effectively in community issues'.[13] He is married with two sons and lives in the leafy precinct of USJ 18.

Soon after arriving in USJ in 1997, Raymond had three pairs of shoes stolen within a single month. When his new neighbours pointed out that petty theft was common in the area, Raymond suggested that they set up a *rukun tetangga*, the Malaysian equivalent of a Neighbourhood Watch scheme. His 'independent-minded' neighbours were reluctant, though, to join a government scheme that is 'often abused for political interests'. Moreover, the scheme had lain dormant for many years and was widely seen as ineffectual. So Raymond turned to the Web for inspiration and found Neighbourhood Watch schemes in Britain, America and Australia to emulate: 'Everything was the same as *rukun tetangga* but without the government. We just repackaged it'.

In 1999 Raymond formed a Neighbourhood Watch committee for USJ 18. Each committee member was entrusted with the task of organising night patrols for a single street in the precinct. In its early 2000s heyday, the scheme boasted 330 volunteer patrollers guarding the precinct's 536 houses. Patrollers walked the streets in pairs carrying batons and mobile phones and were instructed to report any suspicious activity to the police. This regular surveillance practice was strengthened by a programme of local events led by Raymond and aimed at fostering good neighbourly relations.

In May 2001 Raymond's scheme received federal funding under the umbrella of the federal programme DAGS (see Chapter 4). Raymond became the founder and manager of Nwatch.net.my, a web portal devoted to issues of local crime and security. In February 2004 Raymond took me through his online surveillance routines, which at the time he carried out religiously from midnight until around 1 A.M. from his home computer. He started by running the anti-spam application Mailwasher, downloading email from his mailserver and updating his bird flu watch data. He then searched through Malaysia's online news media for crime

Figure 5.2. The Neighbourhood Watch activist and multilevel marketing distributor, Raymond Tan, in a recent photograph. Source: courtesy of Raymond Tan.

news and advice, emailing himself a link on crime prevention from the New Straits Times for future reference. One of his regular tasks is to warn fellow residents of any urban legends, hoaxes or scams that may be circulating through local lists or web forums. Some extortionists 'groom you first [online] and then fly you over to Nigeria'. In addition to this surveillance practice, Raymond uses local mailing lists to send collective seasonal greetings to other local leaders and residents during major celebrations such as Christmas or Chinese New Year.

Raymond puts his personal media (his PC, software, email, mobile devices) to collective uses by aligning his Internet practices with a central concern of local residents: the fear of crime. He achieves this alignment through skilled, embodied, 'seemingly effortless' practices (Moores 2005: 23) of neighbourhood surveillance and conviviality, both onscreen and face-to-face. As Raymond is only too aware, crime is a 'galvanising issue' (Melucci 1996, Venkatesh 2003) that transcends divides of race, religion and ideology and can bring together highly disparate people around a common cause.[14] Alas these leadership activities require time and dedication, and by 2003 other volunteers were privately expressing their concern

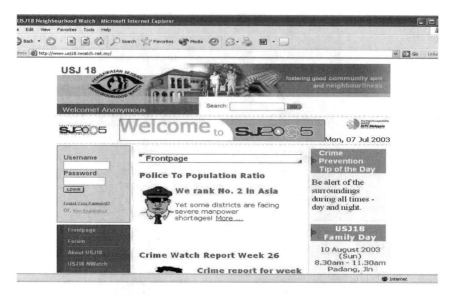

Figure 5.3. A screenshot of the Neighbourhood Watch portal taken on 7 July 2003.

that Raymond's growing business activities were hampering his grass-roots work.

Perhaps to put paid to rumours about his wavering grassroots commitment, in 2004 Raymond led a successful campaign against the building of a food court on land earmarked for the construction of a police station. Mobilising his vast set of ties across the field of residential affairs and using a range of Internet and mobile technologies (email, listservs, web forums, mobile phones) with his associates he swiftly rallied local residents at the construction site in full view of Malaysia's mass media. Following this mobilisation the residents were given official guarantees that a police station would be built on the site.[15] The campaign was spearheaded not by that ghostly fiction known as 'the community' but rather by a small action committee drawn from Raymond's set of local contacts. This ad-hoc committee can be described as an 'action-set', that is, a set of people who are mobilised to achieve a specified goal only to disperse as soon as this goal is attained or abandoned (Mayer 1966, Turner 1974). The work of the action-set was aided by Jeff Ooi's citizen journalism which contributed to the campaign's mass media visibility. Raymond emerged from the campaign not as the 'caged monkey' of activist lore but rather as a formidable field broker with the ability to mobilise local residents at very short notice.

Despite these episodic efforts, by 2005 other crime-prevention leaders had emerged in Subang Jaya alongside Raymond. Thus in February

2005 it was other activists who pioneered the suburb's new 'community SMS alert service'.[16] It was during this period that Raymond became committed to multilevel marketing, described by Sparks and Schenk (2001: 849) as 'networks of member distributors whose earnings come both from selling products and recruiting new members'. At present he is a distributor with USANA Health Sciences, a US-based company that sells personal care and nutritional products. In a 13 December 2008 personal blog entry, Raymond writes about a recent trip to the Philippines, a new market for USANA, and invites prospective business partners in that country to contact him via email. In addition to his personal blog and email, he also makes frequent use of websites, instant messaging, Internet telephony (Skype) and mobile telephony for both business and leisure pursuits – a panoply of interpersonal technologies that he lists in his email signature so as to offer actual and potential contacts a range of options through which they can reach him.

Raymond has taken pains to keep his multilevel marketing and residential activism strictly apart. Thus when he started recruiting distributors in Subang Jaya and USJ he was concerned that he may be seen as taking unfair advantage of his high profile as a grassroots leader for personal financial gain: 'I don't want to be seen to abuse my platform', he told me. For this reason he is always careful not to entangle the two strands of practice when interacting with fellow residents either online or offline. We again witness at work here, as in Jeff Ooi's Harvard incident, the fundamental field law of selfless volunteerism: whilst pursuing one's self-interest through a range of social ties and personal media is perfectly acceptable within the field of multilevel marketing (indeed it is the field's very raison d'être), the opposite is true in the 'inverted economy' (Bourdieu 1996) of the field of residential affairs where one's social and technological capital must serve the common good.

The Weakness of Weak Ties

To recapitulate, all three leaders have exploited very effectively the technical affordances of personal media (interactivity, portability, personalisation) to pursue their public ambitions. Yet we cannot regard their personal media in isolation from collective and mass media (see Lüders 2008 and above). For instance, we saw how Raymond Tan sent himself an email with a newspaper article's URL as an aide-memoire. He did this with a view to sharing helpful information on crime prevention with fellow residents via collective outlets such as his own crimewatch portal or local mailing lists. Within a single, effortless routine action he enlisted three distinctive types of media – personal, collective and mass media – to a communitarian goal. Likewise, when the politician Lee Hwa Beng had his photograph taken by a loyal supporter during local events, the assumption was that the pictures may eventually surface on any number of digital platforms along the personal-group-mass media continuum.

We also saw how all three leaders have used personal media to create, maintain and mobilise a range of weak ties across Subang Jaya's field of residential affairs and beyond. Weak ties were in fact essential to the restructuring of this increasingly Internet-mediated field from the late 1990s, when these leaders and a few others, along with an army of followers, pioneered a series of local innovations around pressing issues affecting residents, such as local taxation, crime, poor governance and ethnic relations. These innovations included news groups, web forums, Neighbourhood Watch schemes, residents' committees and sports tournaments. Thus in 1999 Jeff Ooi used personal media such as email and mobile phones (as well as group and mass media) to mobilise the residents against the council over a sharp rise in local taxes. This led to the creation of the local web portal USJ.com.my which soon became a key site of suburban sociality and residential politics. Subsequently, from 2003, Jeff gathered a flock of 'little birds' or sources (a special subset of weak ties) around his personal blog Screenshots and went on to become Malaysia's leading political blogger. Similarly, from 1999 Raymond Tan has used personal media to cultivate useful weak ties under the ecumenical theme of crime – ties that reach across specialist (sub)fields of practice such as residential affairs, party politics, local government, policing and journalism. In 2004 he successfully mobilised these ties via personal and other media to campaign against the building of a food court on land reserved for a police station. Meanwhile he used personal media (email, mobile phones, instant messaging, Internet telephony) to develop new weak ties in the field of multilevel marketing, both in Malaysia and abroad.

The hybrid field/network analysis also highlighted a key characteristic of weak ties overlooked in previous studies which have emphasised, with Granovetter, the usefulness of such ties (e.g., when seeking employment or business partners). As we saw with Raymond's multilevel marketing efforts and Jeff's Harvard incident, certain kinds of weak ties in certain fields of practice must be handled with care lest they become a liability. The problem lies not so much with the weak ties in themselves but with their public management across social fields. As far as regular practitioners in the field of residential affairs are concerned, local leaders are welcome to have as rich a set of weak ties as they please so long as they do not use them to the detriment of 'the community'. In a media-rich locale such as Subang Jaya, leaders must learn how to manage the public (in)visibility of their weak ties, mobilising certain sets of weak ties for some purposes, demobilising them for others. This management often involves the deft articulation of personal, collective and mass media across social fields that exhibit very different logics, e.g., the fields of party politics, policing and local government. Seen from this perspective, the importance of cross-field issues such as crime becomes even more apparent. These galvanising issues allow leaders such as Raymond or Lee to align entire regions of their personal networks and a range of personal media with the enduring concerns of both specialist practitioners and 'the general public'.

It will be recalled that Amit (2002) regards a personal network as that 'framework of social linkage that requires perhaps the most intensive, self-conscious and constant efforts from its key protagonists, but which is also the most structurally ephemeral'. Personal networks are far more vulnerable than social groups and organisations to the vagaries of the life course (such as illness, migration, employment, divorce) and to historical changes in the wider cultural space in which the agent's life unfolds (e.g., regime changes, economic crises, civil strife). Although personal media can somewhat mitigate or cushion the effects of major life changes (e.g., by allowing a migrant to remain in contact with his/her family, but see Miller 2007) they cannot alter the irreversibility of biological time or make a personal network sustainable beyond ego's biological death.[17] The implications of these inherent constraints of personal networks for the study of personal media and local politics are clearly instantiated in the three profiles above. For a local leader, remaining in contact with local allies and supporters via personal media cannot be a substitute for being regularly co-present 'on the ground' tackling local issues (Coleman 2005). Thus Jeff Ooi's new post as an MP in the northern state of Penang and Raymond's commitment to opening up the Philippine market cannot but reduce their availability for leadership in Subang Jaya. Another example is the political earthquake that shook Malaysia in 2008 which benefitted Jeff the political candidate but not Jeff the local activist, while ousting Lee Hwa Beng despite his back-breaking work over the years.

Conclusion

The combination of a field and network approach to the personal media practices of local leaders in Subang Jaya-USJ has revealed such practices to be inextricable from the social fields in which they take place. Whilst personal media were integral to the restructuring of the field of residential affairs in the suburb from the latter part of the 1990s, no individual leader (regardless of their personal charisma, social capital or technical sophistication) was ever above the sociocentric laws of the field – not even the remarkable political innovators profiled here. In sum, Subang Jaya's field of residential affairs is not fertile ground for the growth of networked individualism.

The analysis was framed not by a vaguely defined 'local community' but rather with reference to a dynamic 'field of residential affairs'. I define such a field as an inverted T-shaped domain of practice in which variously positioned human agents compete and cooperate over local issues through a range of practices and technologies, including personal media. Along the vertical or governmental axis, elected leaders such as Lee Hwa Beng have no choice but to put their personal media at the service of their constituents by ceaselessly going 'down to the ground' (*turun padang*) in order to identify and resolve local issues (Chapter 1). In stark contrast to Wellman's and Castells' 'me-centred' model of networked individualism, Lee's political motto and personal media signature is 'Yours in service'. Meanwhile, along the horizontal or nongovernmental field axis, leaders such as Raymond or Jeff cannot but align their personal media practices with the prevailing collectivist doxa and communitarian media that they themselves were pivotal in creating. As Victor Turner (1974) argued for the failed Mexican revolutionary Miguel Hidalgo, whilst charismatic leaders can mobilise ties from the various fields of practice in which they are active (in Hidalgo's case, across fields as disparate as indigenous cash-cropping, the Catholic Church, the freemasons and the provincial intelligentsia), the resulting action-set cannot be sustained for long, for it will disperse as soon as the common goal is achieved or abandoned (here when Hidalgo was captured and put to death by the Spanish). In the contemporary world, personal media can certainly contribute to the swift mobilisation and micro-coordination of weak ties for collective action – the 'smart mobs' phenomenon (Chadwick 2006, Rafael 2003, Rheingold 2002) – but always under severe social and life-historical constraints.

Notes

1. See the *Guardian Online*, 21 January 2009, http://www.guardian.co.uk/world/2009/jan/21/barack-obama-blackberry-national-security.
2. See Aufderheide (1995), Barber (2006), Bernard (1974), Bilu and Ben-Ari (1992), Bob (2005), Bräuchler (2005), Dickey (1993), Goody (1987), Hinkelbein (2008), Hughes-Freeland (2007), Johnson (2001), Landsman (1987), Peterson (2004), Peterson (2003), Postill (2006), Reis (2008), Scherer (1988), Schulz (2006), Smith

(2006), Strauss (2007), Turner (2002), van de Port (2006) and Warner (1959).

3. http://hwabeng.org.my/node/1176.

4. ADUN (*Ahli Dewan Undangan Negeri*) is the Malay acronym for state assemblyman.

5. Lee used the Malay term *kampong* (village).

6. See *The Economist*, 12 February 2009, http://www.economist.com/specialreports/displaystory.cfm?story_id=13063298.

7. It is easy to forget that Jeff was an active member of the ruling coalition's Gerakan party from 2000 to 2007, before joining the DAP in June 2007.

8. For a similar rhetoric in the Philippines, see Rafael (2003).

9. http://parliament.jeffooi.com/?page_id=2.

10. http://oonyeoh.squarespace.com/chrome/2005/12/3/jeff-ooi-screenshooter.html.

11. http://en.wikipedia.org/wiki/Jeff_Ooi.

12. Julian Hopkins, personal communication, 22 December 2007.

13. Personal communication, 11 March 2009.

14. The implicit (or doxic) assumption is that most local residents are law-abiding, middle-class homeowners, and that the threat to their well-being is likely to come from low-income outsiders, especially foreign immigrants. When I asked another crimewatcher whether he thought the scheme may be helping to perpetuate social inequality, he seemed surprised at the question, but replied that they could not be expected to solve all social ills and that their remit was exclusively crime; there were already dedicated government agencies tackling poverty.

15. The new police station was officially handed over to the police by the developer on 24 March 2009, see http://thestar.com.my/metro/story.asp?file=/2009/3/25/central/3547413&sec=central.

16. Namely Robert Chan, Christopher 'Orchi' Ng and PC Yeoh, see http://www.jeffooi.com/2006/10/crime_alerts_the_usjsubang_jay.php.

17. Cf. Barendregt and Pertierra (2008) on how the dead in Indonesia and the Philippines may at times communicate with the living through mobile phones.

CHAPTER 6

Internet Dramas

In previous chapters I have outlined the formation and consolidation of a new Internet field: the field of residential affairs in Subang Jaya. Alongside such structuring processes, all social fields are subject to sudden crises, some of which may lead to significant changes. But how well equipped is field theory to handle these crises and changes?

The received wisdom about Bourdieu's field theory is that it neglects processes of change and overemphasizes social reproduction. One influential commentator, Richard Jenkins (2002: 95–96), follows Connell (1983) in pointing out that in Bourdieu's field theory process is a 'black box'. This assessment is misleading, though, on three counts. First, as Jenkins himself notes (2002: 96), Bourdieu does devote a great deal of attention to the processual aspects of walking, sitting, conversing, and so on – what he calls 'bodily hexis'. Second, Bourdieu's most fully developed exposition of field theory, *The Rules of Art* (1996), is nothing if not the detailed study of an unfolding historical process: the growing autonomisation of the field of art in nineteenth-century France. Third, and most germane to the argument I am pursuing here, there is one other family of processes not mentioned by Jenkins that Bourdieu's field theory does indeed consign to a black box: political processes.

Take Bourdieu's (1996: 52) account of Flaubert's famous *Madame Bovary* trial, where the novelist stood accused of publishing immoral materials. At the time of the trial, the Parisian salons, says Bourdieu, became sites for mobilisation in support of Flaubert. Bourdieu mentions in passing this episode to illustrate the importance of the salons as points of articulation between the fields of art, commerce and government, distinguished more by who they excluded than by who they included (1996: 51–53). Yet he does not consider the trial to be a political process worthy of detailed analysis in its own right. Instead, Bourdieu's analytical preference is for the slow-moving, cumulative changes that take place *within* a field (Swartz 1997: 129; Couldry 2003), not for potentially volatile, unpredictable processes such as trials that often migrate across fields (my second case study below is one such example of a migratory process). In contrast, the Parisian salons, brasseries and courthouses provide Bourdieu with a relatively fixed spatial matrix of objective relations – a socio-physical backdrop to a slowly changing field of practice (see Bourdieu 1996: 40–43).

Social Dramas

Political processes were, in fact, central to the collaborative work of a group of anthropologists known as the Manchester School (see Chapters 1 and 2) whose field theories predate Bourdieu's by several decades. By political process they meant that kind of social process that is 'involved in determining and implementing public goals [as well as] in the differential achievement and use of power by the members of the group concerned with those goals' (Swartz et al. 1966: 7).

One key Manchester School concept is 'social drama'. Coined by the other major field theorist besides Bourdieu, Victor Turner, a social drama is a political process that originates within a social group but can spread across a wider inter-group field unless appropriate 'redressive action' is taken (Turner 1974: 128–32). In 2003 and 2004, the field of residential affairs in Subang Jaya went through at least two social dramas, the second of which was widely covered by the Malaysian mass media. These dramas provide us with an insight into how local activists are appropriating the Internet to pursue their aims, in effect 'localizing' the Internet. They also reveal the workings of the laws of *turun padang* and volunteerism – introduced in Chapter 1 – and their effects on the various processes of Internet localization. Social dramas usually unfold around crises in the political lives of influential individuals and point at structural contradictions within the group or broader social field. In his classic monograph *Schism and Continuity in an African Society* (1996), originally published in 1957, Turner explored the structural contradiction among the Ndembu of Zambia between virilocal residence and matrilineal descent. While among patrilineal groups inheritance, succession and group membership come under a single principle, matrilineal groups use different principles for different rights and duties (Eriksen and Nielsen 2001: 98).

Social dramas undergo four stages: (1) breach, (2) crisis, (3) redressive action, and (4) reintegration or schism. First, there is a 'breach of regular norm-governed social relations', for example an aspiring

Ndembu leader repeatedly failing to show respect towards his elders. This breach may give way to a stage of 'mounting crisis' that could rapidly spiral out of control. Crises are of special analytical value as, according to Turner, they reveal the state of a group's factionalism. Beneath the turbulence of dispute, an embedded – yet slowly changing – social structure becomes visible. This structure is made up of fairly constant social relations. The post-crisis stage opens when the group's leaders activate both formal and informal redressive mechanisms. These can vary greatly depending on the depth and social significance of the breach, the nature of the group, the group's degree of autonomy from 'wider systems of social relations', and so on. The final stage is reached when the disputing parties either return to the fold or go their separate ways. While established societies will have legal or ritual institutions designed to handle breaches, new groups lacking such institutions will be prone to fission (Turner 1996: 91–115, cf. Skinner 2009).

In addition to the notion of social drama, I will draw on a less well-known Turnerian concept, namely 'arena' (Turner 1974: 132–36). Arenas are the actual physical settings where social dramas unfold; traditionally streets, battlefields or courtrooms, but extending in our current era to TV studios, Facebook groups or Twitter trends. To stress the increasingly complex Internet mediations at work in the two dramas analysed, I will use the term 'Internet drama' (cf. Wagner-Pacifici 1986, Eyerman 2008).

Drama I: 'Use your Brain, Clear this Drain!'

Breach
This Internet drama was triggered by a breach of the regular norms governing relations between residents' groups and the municipal council. The drama started on 13 June 2004 when the founder and leader of the Subang Jaya e-Community Portal (USJ.com.my), Jeff Ooi, came across a photograph in the Mandarin-language press in which a small group of residents, myself included, were demonstrating behind a banner bearing the web portal's domain name. We were protesting against the council's inaction following the collapse of a drain's retaining wall. Councillor Yap, the state assemblyman Lee Hwa Beng's right hand, had *turun padang* ('gone down the ground') and called the press to draw attention to the plight of Lee's constituents. Jeff was incensed at the misuse of the domain name on a banner whose text contained what all agreed was an insulting remark hurled at the council (MPSJ), namely 'USE YOUR BRAIN CLEAR THIS DRAIN!'. He then translated his anger into a front page editorial on the web portal under the headline: 'WE DESERVE A PUBLIC APOLOGY'.

The editorial showed the offending picture and demanded an apology from the culprits within seventy-two hours (Figures 6.1 and 6.2).

Figure 6.1. This photograph, published in the Chinese-language press, incensed the owner of the Subang Jaya e-Community Portal, Jeff Ooi, for its misuse of the portal's domain name (USJ.com.my) on a banner whose bilingual text contained an insulting remark hurled at the council (MPSJ), namely 'USE YOUR BRAIN CLEAR THIS DRAIN!'.

Crisis

Jeff also started a discussion thread on the topic, thereby opening up the web forum as the main arena where the social drama unfolded. An arena is a 'bounded spatial unit in which precise, visible antagonists, individual or corporate, contend with one another for prizes and/or honor' (Turner 1974: 132–33). It is an 'explicit frame' in which 'nothing is left merely implied' and major decisions are taken (1974: 134). To the field theorist, it is an opportunity to study the field at close range. Throughout the crisis, Jeff and his forum co-administrator, KW Chang, ensured that nothing remained 'merely implied'. In addition to demanding an apology, they repeatedly asked forum participants to clarify comments or insinuations they had made in previous posts. For instance, one of the demonstrators was asked to clarify an 'amazing' comment in which he appeared to present himself as a forum moderator, when in fact he enjoyed no such status. Another participant was asked to explain his insinuation that Jeff feared that the demonstration may frustrate his secret plan to sell off the portal to the local council – a rumour that had been circulating offline for some time. He also 'flamed' Jeff for bragging about his international profile as a blogger and e-Community activist invited to speak at Harvard University and was duly reprimanded. It will be recalled from Chapter 5 that this forum user had reached out for the egalitarian rhetoric of 'community'. Here are some expanded extracts from his post:

> usj.com.my is a community website (unless i am wrong). It is NOT a primary site as intellectual forum for show offs, wannabes and what nots.

> a community web site serves the needs and wants of a community. it assist the residents to voice its opinions and overcome obstacles or red tapes. It should assist and solves pcommunity problems.

> The target audience, the subang jaya residents (me for e.g.) is interested in using usj.com.my to assist in making subang jaya a better place to live in.

> I do not give a flying banana about mit, oxford or harvard talk. I have that already in the office and in any half decent pubs.

A third contributor adopted a more diplomatic tone to express his concern that the once proudly independent forum may have become 'tamed'. Throughout the crisis, Jeff's position was clear and consistent. He insisted that with independence comes responsibility, and that there was much more at stake than a mere clogged drain. At stake was the long-term prospect of 'building bridges' with the local council towards a democratic partnership and a Knowledge Society.

Redressive Action and Reintegration
At any rate, the crisis was overcome through what Turner (1996: 91) calls 'redressive action': heartfelt apologies were extended to the council and the offenders eventually returned to the forum after a voluntary 'cooling off' period (Turner's 'reintegration'). Meanwhile, Jeff had introduced a new set of forum rules and regulations to ensure that 'mature' forms of online communication prevailed. Initially some of the regular contributors found these rules constraining, but over the course of the next few months it became clear that there was still ample room for manoeuvre on the forum.

Implications
As with Turner's Ndembu villagers, this social drama reveals a key structural contradiction within the field of residential affairs in Subang Jaya

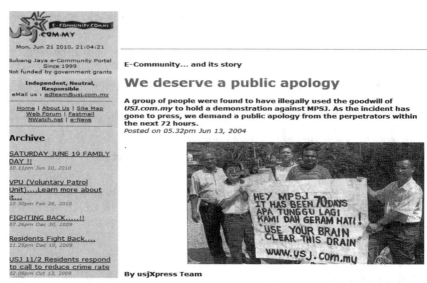

By usjXpress Team

Figure 6.2. Jeff Ooi precipitated an Internet drama within the field of residential affairs in Subang Jaya with this editorial demanding a public apology from a group of residents who had used abusive language against the local council and signed their banner with his portal's domain name.[1]

(and perhaps elsewhere). Here the contradiction has to do not with kinship but rather with status. The dogged egalitarianism of the residential field is at odds with distinctions of status and power that derive from other fields yet cannot but percolate into the field. This explains why those residents who are thought to be boasting about their extra-field achievements (e.g., having been invited to speak at Harvard) have to be brought back down to the *padang*.[2] There are two further problems. First, even in the most egalitarian of small-scale societies, distinctions of status, ability and achievement are both inevitable and publicly indexed in social practice and convention. We saw a clear example of this when a forum participant was scolded for assuming the role of moderator when in reality he was a mere subscriber. Second, and to use Bourdieu's metaphor of capital, exchanging currencies obtained in other fields is a complicated business for leading residents. Whereas powerful outsiders such as the state assemblyman are allowed, indeed expected, to convert financial capital – euphemistically known as 'sponsorship' – into symbolic capital in order to assist 'the community', residents like Jeff Ooi place themselves in a difficult position when they do the same (e.g., by part-funding the web portal himself). As we said in Chapter 1, the fundamental field law for residents states that they must donate their spare time, not their spare money, for the collective good of fellow residents. To accumulate symbolic capital, residents must visibly support 'the community' through disinterested acts of generosity in the form of voluntary work, useful advice, and such like. As in the fields of art and Christian charity described by Bourdieu (1993, 1998), local activists have developed a vested 'interest in disinterestedness'. Any activist suspected of abusing his position for personal financial gain must be prepared to face online challenges.

Drama II: 'We want a Police Station!'

I will now turn to an Internet drama of greater complexity and much wider ramifications than the episode just analysed. If in the latter drama Jeff Ooi succeeded in limiting the potential damage to intra-field relations, in this second crisis he joined forces with other activists to spread the crisis well beyond the regular bounds of the residential field, reaching all the way up to Malaysia's highest corridors of political and media power. This second drama revolved around the building of a food court on land reserved for a police station and was triggered once again by a perceived breach of the regular norms governing relations between the residents and the local council.

Breach
The drama began on Wednesday 22 September 2004 at 4:57 P.M. when Raymond Tan, the Neighbourhood Watch activist, started a thread on the USJ. com.my main web forum entitled 'A new balai?' (*balai polis* is the Malay term for police station). The contents of that first posting were also sent to subscribers of USJ.com.my's news group under the heading 'A new police station?':

> From: Raymond Tan
> To: usj_subangjaya@yahoogroups.com
> Sent: Wednesday, September 22, 2004 4:57 PM
> Subject: [uSJ NewsGroup] A new police station?
>
> The construction has just started but sorry to disappoint you, folks. It isn't for a new balai that we have been asking for! The land which we understand to be reserved for the future expansion of the existing mini-balai in USJ8 has instead being leased out to a private individual who has sub-leased it to Pack Connexion Sdn. Bhd., to be turned into a food court. This food court will be called Subang Food Garden with 107 food stalls, e.g., 35 for halal food and 72 for non-halal food. Operating hours will be from 5pm to 3am or 7am to 3am, subject to confirmation. What do you feel about this new development? We have created a quick poll to solicit your response. Go to www.nwatch.net.my to cast your vote!

As was the case here, Raymond frequently uses mailing lists to direct subscribers to his Nwatch portal. The aim of the poll was, of course, to mobilise residents against an imputed breach of the council's duty to serve the ratepayers, with the implication of a hidden profit motive. The following day another well-known activist replied both to the USJ. com.my web forum and to the mailing list suggesting that there may be 'somebody in MPSJ promoting Food Courts in SJ/USJ'. The fact that the land was reserved for a police station made the issue 'even fishier'.

Crisis
By Saturday 25 September the discussion had spread to other local mailing lists. In an email sent to five mailing lists across the porous government/ non-government divide separating residents' groups, a local resident asked for advice on the recently launched campaign to text local MPs and state assemblymen via SMS protesting the building of the food court. This person had received an SMS reply from the state assemblyman, Lee Hwa Beng, suggesting that they contact the council directly (the same response had been reported by a web forum poster the day before). Raymond replied by encouraging others to feed the politicians' responses back to the mailing list, or alternatively to either the Nwatch or USJ.com.my portals. With hindsight, this request was an early indication that a formidable cross-field alliance was in the making. Meanwhile, on the USJ.com.my web forum, Raymond's *balai* thread was growing rapidly. One participant had suggested that all major residents' groups be informed of the campaign, to which Raymond replied: 'worry not – OUR relevant platforms are in constant contact with each other. Right now, all we need most is PEOPLE POWER!'

On Sunday 26 September, Jeff Ooi sent subscribers of all five mailing lists a piece he had recently posted on the portal's news section (Figure 6.3). The headline left no doubt as to the item's mobilising intent: 'Stop the FOOD-COURT mania!' The piece chided the members of parliament and assemblymen for 'keep[ing] mum on the progress of their job to relay the resident's protest to the local council'. It then noted the absence of a project notice board at the building site, 'mandatory of all the erection of new holdings'. This remark resonates with reports of local activism from elsewhere. Faced with powerful interests, people around the world 'have quickly invented resourceful means of resistance' (Abram 1998: 13). Thus, local activists in France 'check whether planning procedures have been correctly followed'. Should any 'procedural lapses' be identified, 'the project can be challenged in the administrative court and any further planning or development works suspended' (Newman 1994: 220, quoted in Abram 1998: 13).

Mon, Jun 21 2010, 21:19:22

Subang Jaya e-Community Portal
Since 1999
Not funded by government grants

Independent, Neutral,
Responsible
eMail us : edteam@usj.com.my

Home | About Us | Site Map
Web Forum | Fastmail
NWatch.net | e-News

Archive

E-Community... and its story

Stop the food-court mania!

Will USJ police station be further delayed? Residents are up in arms as they learned precious land reserved for a full-sized police station has been leased "5 years + 5 years" to build a food-court that will operate till 3.00am everyday.
Posted on 05.14pm Sep 26, 2004

By usjXpress team
Email: edteam@usj.com.my

Subang Jaya, September 26:

Promoters of foodcourt projects are eyeing depleting prime land around USJ, no matter they are designated open spaces for the residents or part of the police station's reserved land.

Figure 6.3. On this occasion, Jeff Ooi confronts the municipal council head-on by lending his editorial support to a campaign aimed at preventing the building of a food court on land reserved for a police station. The campaign was orchestrated by an action-set led by Raymond Tan.[3]

That same day, Raymond announced the recent formation of an S.O.B. (Save Our Balai) Action Committee both on the web forum and in an email to all five mailing lists. In an unusually strongly worded pun, the stated aim was to 'Save our Balai … from some greedy SOBs who see it fit to sacrifice public interests for other purposes'. He then listed the names and affiliations of the pro tem committee members, with himself at the helm as Protem Chairman and his Nwatch right hand, Robert Chan, as Deputy Chairman. The other eleven members were recruited from across the field of residential affairs, including Nwatch, the council's residents' committees (JKPs) and the independent but sleepy USJ Residents' Association (USJRA). In keeping with the direct appeal character of the campaign, Raymond ended his email with a call to action: 'Our meeting notes will be posted in this forum shortly. Can we count on your support?' As I noted in Chapter 5, the campaign was spearheaded not by an imaginary 'community' but rather by a subset of Raymond's local contacts in the shape of a small action committee. This improvised committee is best described as an 'action-set', i.e., a set of individuals mobilised to attain a specified goal who will disperse when that goal is either reached or abandoned (Mayer 1966, Turner 1974).

On 27 September, Raymond's close ally, Robert Chan, informed web forum subscribers that the campaign to lobby MPs and assemblymen via SMS had 'resulted in jolting each and every one of them into action'. Robert appended a list of local politicians and their reactions to the texted messages, which ranged from 'full support' to a promise to 'look into the matter'. Here we can see clearly Turner's arena principles at work through a new technological articulation, that between Internet and mobile media. Nothing must be left unsaid; all actors drawn into the drama ('jolted into action') must state publicly where they stand on the dispute at hand.

The following day, Raymond contributed a web and listserv posting in which he identified, like the French activists mentioned earlier, a number of procedural lapses in the food court project: 'But what baffles is how this application could be approved without the green light from Licensing. Fishy, fishy, fishy'. Furthermore, no application had been made to the Engineering Committee, responsible for approving all building work. All this suggested there may be '[a] higher power at play'. That same day, a resident reported on the Nwatch forum having received the following SMS from the state assemblyman, Lee Hwa Beng: 'MPSJ had issued a stop work order last Friday. Shall follow up till work stop. Agree the hawker ctr is not suitable. Should built police station only – Hwa Beng'.

On 3 October the drama's central arena shifted offline when some two hundred residents (a large gathering by local standards) demonstrated peacefully at the building site 'under full media coverage', as Raymond put it. Simultaneously, the S.O.B. Action Committee released a statement to the press 'Just to make sure that we do not get misquoted'. This statement signals both the activists' learning from past experience and the field's gradual maturation and autonomisation from the fields of journalism and government.

Redressive Action

The climax of the drama came on 4 October, when the Deputy Home Minister Datuk Noh Omar paid a visit to USJ (Subang Jaya). Raymond's emotive web announcement captures a rare moment of jubilation, a fleeting moment when the structural contradiction between the laws of *turun padang* and volunteerism was held in abeyance:

We disagreed. We came together. He heard. And he turun padang.

Friends and neighbours, Our Timbalan Menteri Keselamatan Dalam Negeri YB Dato' Noh Omar made a personal visit to USJ 8 Pondok Polis about noon time. After hearing views from all parties concerned (including the operator's rep), he decided that the food court is a 'no-go' and he directed the operator to withdraw the application or he will get Bukit Aman to revoke the lease agreement. He also promised to look into the construction of a new balai by 2005/2006.

Congratulations, folks!

Tune in to RTM and TV3 tonight!

This redressive action by the federal authorities was soon reciprocated by the local activists, who were only too eager, as one of them put it, to 'complete the cycle' of the campaign. To this end, the S.O.B. deputy leader, Robert Chan, circulated a message asking residents to show their elected representatives their gratitude by sending them an SMS with the text: 'Thank you for helping us get back our Balai Polis'.

Reintegration?

Yet only two months after these auspicious events, in December 2004, fresh rumours began to circulate online that the operator was planning to resume construction of the food court. On 16 February 2005, the local council approved the project, and physical work reportedly resumed at the site on 18 February. Raymond's reaction was: 'Friends and neighbours, are we going to allow these clowns [to] push the FOOD court down our throats?'

There is no space here to discuss the subsequent unfolding of events, which included a highly unusual offline arena, namely a public hearing held on 26 March 2005.[5] Eighteen months after this hearing, activists were reasonably optimistic that the police station would be built with funds from the forthcoming 9th Malaysian Plan. They were not, however, claiming victory just yet. Eventually the police station was completed on 24 March 2009, after nearly a five-year wait.

Implications

This drama demonstrates further the limitations of the community/ network paradigm for the study of Internet localization (Chapter 2). By broadening out the analysis from the neighbourhood domain to the wider field of residential affairs in which Raymond Tan operates, we have gained further insights into his individual agency, his relations with other local agents, and the multiple uses of Internet technologies by activists at a critical point in the suburb's history.

Raymond emerged from this drama not as the 'caged monkey' he was made out to be after he accepted public funds but rather as a formidable field broker (Chapter 5). Like local cyberactivists in other parts of the world, Raymond possesses 'an unusual combination of technical, po-

Subang Jaya e-Community Portal
Since 1999
Not funded by government grants

Independent, Neutral, Responsible
eMail us : edteam@usj.com.my

Home | About Us | Site Map
Web Forum | Fastmail
NWatch.net | e-News

Archive

SATURDAY JUNE 19 FAMILY DAY !!
10.11pm Jun 10, 2010

VPU (Voluntary Patrol Unit)....Learn more about it...
10.30pm Feb 26, 2010

FIGHTING BACK.....!!
07.26pm Dec 30, 2009

Residents Fight Back....
11.25pm Dec 18, 2009

E-Community... and its story

'People's Order' for now!

USJ residents are fed-up that MPSJ's 'STOP-WORK' and 'DEMOLITION' orders that have been issued but took no effect on the foodcourt developer. October 3, hundreds of residents staged a peaceful protest...
Give us our Balai Polis!
Posted on 01.50am Oct 04, 2004

By usjXpress team
Email: edteam@usj.com.my

Subang Jaya, October 3:

Fed up with talks of MPSJ's 'STOP-WORK' and 'demolition orders, USJ residents came out by the hundreds Sunday morning to stage a peaceful protest.

Figure 6.4. A local Member of Parliament shakes hands with the Internet activist Raymond Tan while they hold a copy of a residents' statement opposing the construction of a food court[4]

litical and cultural skills' (Coleman 2004: 39) – skills which he hones not only online, for they are still 'highly dependent upon face-to-face contact' (2004: 39). Throughout the Internet drama, he connected and coordinated the disparate parties involved (activists, politicians, civil servants and journalists) using a range of Internet and telephone technologies as well as face-to-face encounters. At least five mailing lists, two web forums, personal email and mobile telephony were recruited to the intensive campaigning. Two key 'Internet affordances' (Wellman et al. 2003) were exploited to the full, namely hypertextuality and interactivity. Whilst the widely circulated hyperlinks ensured a high degree of message redundancy, the interactive web forum and email threads aided the active participation of residents in the fast-moving drama. The effect was magnified by the high-quality grassroots journalism of Jeff Ooi and by the ample mass media coverage. Crucially for the history of local activism in the township (and indeed in Malaysia), four residents' groups – ranging from the self-funded through the federal-funded to the local council-funded – came together for the first time to fight a common cause.

By incorporating into the analysis of this episode anthropological notions such as field, arena, and action-set, as well as folk notions such as *turun padang*, I was able to reach beyond the 'specialized mythology' (Appadurai 1986) of Raymond's neighbourhood. More importantly, I could counter the gravitational pull of community and network as the paradigmatic notions in the study of Internet localization. Under conditions of rapid social and technological change, with 'settlers' arriving at suburban frontiers at the same time as the Internet and other new social technologies, it is no coincidence that anthropological notions arising from fieldwork with African urban settlers in the 1950s are still relevant today (see Werbner 1990, Kapferer 2005). Like rural migrants in the booming urban settlements of postwar Africa (Epstein 1958), present-day suburbanites in Malaysia find themselves in densely populated settlements with inadequate social and public facilities. The result is the emergence of ephemeral action-sets seeking to address pressing problems as a matter of urgency (Figure 6.4). Unlike the poor African migrants of previous generations, however, today's middle-income Malaysians have access to a wealth of modern cultural capital and digital technologies. This latter episode illustrates their aggregated, Internet-mediated agency in the face of the state's failure to provide for their perceived surveillance needs.

Bourdieu's Black Box

This chapter has examined a 'black box' in Bourdieu's field theory: not process in general (*pace* Jenkins 2002: 95–96) but more specifically *political* process. This was precisely the emphasis of much earlier work on field theory than Bourdieu's carried out by the Manchester School of Anthropology in Central and Southern Africa. The discussion drew on Victor Turner's field concepts, chiefly social drama and arena, to analyse two Internet dramas that unfolded in Subang Jaya's field of residential affairs in 2004. The first crisis was small: influential residents managed to contain it largely within a single field sub-sector (the Subang Jaya e-Community forum), preventing it from spreading to other field sectors and beyond. In stark contrast, the second crisis spread very rapidly, spilling over into the powerful fields of federal government and the national mass media through the deft use of a range of Internet and mobile technologies by an unprecedented alliance of residents' groups. Residents were protesting against the building of a food court on land reserved for a police station. Together, both crises revealed the field's dynamics of factionalism, alliance-building and Internet mediation, as well as its entanglements with powerful neighbouring fields at two specific points in time.

Notes

1. http://www.usj.com.my/usjXpress/details.php3?table=usjXpress&ID=357.
2. An interesting parallel can be noted here with Britain's House of Lords where, according to the anthropologist Emma Crewe (2005), peers are treated literally

'as peers' regardless of their status outside the House.

3.   http://www.usj.com.my/usjXpress/details.php3?table=usjXpress&ID=363.
4.   http://www.usj.com.my/usjXpress/details.php3?table=usjXpress&ID=366.
5.   http://www.usj.com.my/usjXpress/details.php3?table=usjXpress&ID=380.

CHAPTER 7

Residential Socialities

On 2 July 2004 I joined a group of regular e-Community forum participants (or 'forumers' as they are called) on their monthly get-together
over a *teh tarik*, a tea beverage popular in Peninsular Malaysia. I was
already at the *mamak* coffee shop when the others started to arrive as I
had been interviewing a regular forumer, Patrick Tan, about the early
days in Subang Jaya. With the others we joked about why PC Yeoh always
arrives late. When PC finally turned up he told us a story about a VIP
in Petaling Jaya who once arrived late at a meeting just down the road
from his place. He had kept waiting a poor devil who had rushed all the
way from Singapore to see him. I was hoping we would talk about the
weather, as I had proposed on a forum thread, to avoid reliving England's recent defeat in the European Football Championship against
Portugal. Instead we talked about the previous month's banner incident
(see Chapter 6, Drama I) – another uncomfortable subject for me as I
had got caught in the middle and was seen to have 'washed my hands'
of my fellow demonstrators.

A little later Christopher 'Orchi' Ng asked me a painful question.
Orchi is famous for his inimitable forum posts written in self-parodying,
third-person 'Manglish' ('Err … met up with a couple of seasoned forumers last night for the regular cuppa TT … as Orchi got there earlier
… it was late n Orchi felt a tinch of sleepiness … so Orchi ordered a
glass of kopi-o ice'). He asked me about a thread I had started some
time ago. In an attempt to make my fieldwork more 'reflexive' and 'participatory' I had started a forum thread in the form of a field diary and
invited audience participation. Orchi hit the nail on the head when he
asked me in front of the entire *teh tarik* congregation: 'Err … John …
my fren … don't you feel like you're talking to yourself in your thread?'
Feeling rather inadequate, I had to agree with him, for my thread had

generated little interest and that was exactly how it felt. Fortunately the conversation soon moved on to the unusually quiet state of the forum following the banner incident. Now that the administrators had introduced a barrage of new rules, the feeling was that the forum may never regain its former gregarious glory. Eventually it did recover, however – except for my thread which rapidly faded into oblivion.

The lesson for me was clear. The forum had its own character, its own form of convivial sociality based on polylogical conversation, not diary-like soliloquies. In this chapter I explore this and other forms of residential sociality in Subang Jaya that have arisen in and around the field of residential affairs. My argument is that social fields do not necessarily exhibit a homogenous 'field sociality'. This is certainly the case with Subang Jaya's field of residential affairs where a plurality of socialities have emerged over time. The perils of reducing sociality to totalising categories such as 'field sociality' or 'community sociality' are apparent in Andreas Wittel's (2001) discussion of the new media industry in London. Wittel distinguishes two broad kinds of sociality: community vs. network sociality. Community sociality is the pre-modern, sluggish sociality of physically localised collectivities. By contrast, network sociality is fast-paced and based on fleeting, instrumental encounters (e.g., speed-dating) with a large set of 'contacts'. Young urban professionals working in the new media industries epitomise this latter form of sociality, which Wittel (adapting Wellman and Castells, see Chapter 5) regards as the defining sociality of our era.

The trouble with Wittel's notion of network sociality is that it glosses over notable differences in how people interact with one another within the same field of practice, for example the new media industry in London. Surely the quality of a social interaction within a speed-dating session differs markedly from that in the office canteen or in a board meeting? How do media industry workers in London navigate these different 'field stations' (Chapter 1) while pursuing their goals (advancing their careers, socialising, mating, and so on)? These questions cannot be answered unless we develop a more nuanced understanding of sociality.

Below I unpack the notion of sociality ethnographically, suggesting that it cannot be reduced to a community vs. network binary. Instead I am suggesting that researchers need to approach this question with an open mind, with the expectation that sociality may take on plural forms even within a single universe of practice. The three distinct forms of field sociality that I discuss are committee sociality, patrol sociality, and (web forum) thread sociality. (Other emergent forms that I have no space to discuss here would include ritual sociality, street party sociality, and sporting sociality). Below I discuss their specificities in terms of their type of interaction, mode of discourse and field articulations. It is only through these fine-grained distinctions derived from empirical research on the ground, I suggest, that we can begin to theorise the elusive relationship between Internet practices and the emergence of new forms of residential sociality.

Committee Sociality

In her rich ethnography of the first Palestinian intifada or 'uprising' against the Israelis (1987–1992), Iris Jean-Klein (2003) goes against the grain of the regional literature by suggesting that the socialities of intifada houses and committees are closely intertwined. Whilst in the existing literature committee sociality is used instrumentally as a metonym for Palestinian sociality writ large, for Jean-Klein this kind of small-scale sociality is worthy of analytical attention in its own right (2003: 557). Despite the prominence of committees within social and political activism worldwide, 'the sociality of committees themselves has remained a largely unseen ethnographic object' (2003: 557).

My account of committee sociality is based on participant observation at a number of meetings in Subang Jaya and USJ. As explained in Chapter 4, the JKP or residents' committees system was launched in February 2001 by the municipal council. The then council president, Ahmad Fuad, linked the pioneering scheme to Local Agenda 21, a United Nations programme aimed at improving local governance around the globe. Fuad used the public rhetoric of community to call on 'the involvement of the community as a whole' in the new initiative. In practice, however, until changes were introduced in 2008 all committee members were political appointees. In his desire to 'delegate some authority to the people', Fuad launched a plan to allocate 100,000 ringgits (29,000 US dollars) annually to each of the twenty-four committees 'for small and immediate projects' such as drain repairs or tree-cutting (Yeoh 2005).

Residents' committee sociality is the co-present, synchronous sociality of monthly meetings devoted to discussing local issues (cf. Jean-Klein 2003). Meetings are held at night in air-conditioned rooms and attendance is restricted to committee members and their guests. The bodily orientation is primarily face-to-face – although this will depend on interlocutors' seating positions relative to one another (Pink 2008). Food and drinks are usually provided and consumed in the room during the break. These 'ephemeral items … live on in the form of the social relations that they produce, and which are in turn responsible for reproducing the comestibles' (Gell 1986: 112). The discourse is oral, polylogical and gesturally rich but it is also mediated by texts, most of them shared over the Internet (e.g., the agenda, emails, letters, websites). A committee meeting is therefore both a 'literacy event' (Street 2000) and an Internet-related practice. Albeit a largely sedentary activity, attendants undertake a metaphorical journey whose itinerary is the agenda. It is the task of the chair to 'bring to order' participants who stray too far from this discursive itinerary (Pink 2008). These sessions are deliberative in that participants aim at reaching consensual decisions.[1] Even though meetings are held behind closed doors, minutes are in principle open to all local residents for inspection.

As regards the committees' articulation with the rest of the field of residential affairs, these are hybrid organisations located on the border between the field's governmental and non-governmental sectors. This ambiguous location is a perennial source of friction. The predominant mood at these sessions is neither one of open conflict nor one of fellowship. Instead, there prevails an atmosphere of frustration with the council's seeming inability to solve but a fraction of the myriad issues brought to the table. As one chair put it once during a meeting: 'But what is it we're doing? We cannot just come to meetings!'

Patrol Sociality

Patrolling the streets springs from a deep-seated fear of crime in the severely under-policed suburb. As recounted in previous chapters, in 1999 a Neighbourhood Watch committee was formed in the precinct of USJ 18. Each member was entrusted with organising night patrols for a single street. In its heyday, the scheme had 330 volunteer patrollers – virtually all of them middle-aged men – guarding over the precinct's 536 houses. Night patrol sociality is the side-by-side (not face-to-face) outdoors sociality of the night beat, when volunteer patrollers take time out to walk the streets in pairs.

Patrollers carry torches, whistles, batons or long sticks, mobile phones, pen and paper.[2] The discourse is oral, informal and does not follow a scripted agenda. It is also gesturally poor on account of patrollers' collateral bodily orientation and the nocturnal conditions. Because of the physical and cognitive constraints of verbal discourse (Hutchins 1995), the two partners take it in turns to carry forth the single conversational thread. In keeping with the dyadic nature of patrols, the discourse is dialogical rather than polylogical (see Mulkay 1985). Unlike the discourse of committees, patrol discourse is non-deliberative, unrecorded and private.

As for its field articulations, post-2001 patrolling was tied to an arrangement between local residents, the police and the National IT Council (NITC) who seed-funded a Neighbourhood Watch web portal under the SJ2005 umbrella (Chapter 4). Despite this governmental connection, patrolling itself is largely free from the political tensions and frustrations that beset committee meetings. The mood is one of camaraderie and fellowship – the shoulder-to-shoulder fellowship of the beat. While committee members live off meagre extrinsic rewards (i.e., the occasional resolution of an issue), patrolling is a rewarding activity in its own right that epitomises the fundamental field law of selfless volunteerism (on the intrinsic rewards of practice, see Warde 2005).

Vered Amit's 'trouble with community' as an anthropological concept (Amit and Rapport 2002) is once again pertinent here (Chapter 2). Amit (2002b) illustrates these difficulties through the ethnographic research of Noel Dyck (2002) in suburban British Columbia (Canada). On one occasion, a group of parents and children travelled together by coach to participate in a sports event south of the border in Seattle. This journey was fondly remembered, yet the group could hardly be described as 'a community'. The trip was a one-off, ephemeral social occasion rather than the genesis of an enduring collectivity. Amit's 'sense of contextual fellowship' is captured in the following online comment from a resident in a USJ precinct where night patrols had been discontinued (in this instance such a fellowship is subordinated to the ideal of good neighbourliness):

> Please correct me if I am wrong but … by handing over the neigbourhood [sic] security matters to the professional hired security guards, we have become complacent and have gone back to our usual 'couldn't care less' attitudes.

> I am sure that some of us (if not most of us) have forgotten the times when we had the Night watch patrols done by the residents ourselves. In doing our own patrols, we have gotten to know one another, learnt a bit about our neighbours and most importantly, learnt how to be good neighbours and friends.

Thread Sociality

As mentioned in Chapter 5, after securing federal funding in August 2001 the local resident Raymond Tan set up Nwatch.net.my, a web portal devoted to crime prevention. One prominent area of the portal is the web forum. All local residents with a valid username and password can, in principle, participate – although an assumed command of the English language weeds out many low-income residents (who are less likely, in any case, to have the necessary ICT skills and access to a home computer). This is, nonetheless, an underutilised resource even amongst the middle-class majority. As of 20 March 2006 it had archived a mere 374 threads (topics) and 1,202 postings after six years in existence. This contrasts markedly with the main forum at USJ.com.my, appropriately named 'The Web Forum'. This latter forum had clocked a staggering 5,221 threads and close to 90,000 posts by that same date. Three years later, in March 2009, this had increased to approximately 21,000 threads, 325,000 posts and 26,000 registered members – and by 25 August 2009 the figures were 22,727 threads, 344,634 posts and 30,754 members. Having to grow in the shadow of its exuberant rival, Nwatch's web forum has languished – as indeed have the e-JKP forum and all specialist sub-forums on the USJ.com.my portal itself.

One telltale sign of the relatively low rate of participation at Nwatch. net.my is the fact that most threads are started by its moderators. The explanation for this low usage lies is the nature and limited scope of the topic: crime. Crime lends itself more readily to practical interventions such as patrolling or to factual information-sharing than it does to open-ended conversation, banter or debate. In contrast, Subang Jaya e-Community's main forum is open to any topic, so long as participants tread with care on Malaysia's most 'sensitive' of subjects, namely the constitutional privileges enjoyed by the Malays and their religion, Islam. The result is a highly competitive milieu in which thread starters compete to 'pull the crowds' to their own threads by choosing topical issues.

In contrast to the gesturally rich committee meetings, thread sociality relies on emoticons and avatars to compensate for the reduced bodily cues of online communication (*pace* Hine 2000: 14–27). As noted in connection to suburban Israeli mailing lists (Mesch and Levanon 2003), the asynchronicity of Internet communication allows busy suburbanites to participate on web forums at their own leisure. The following exchange captures the informal, colloquial nature of most threads, as well as the idiosyncratic style of one of the forum's 'stars', Orchi. Notice how Orchi peppers his post with Malay (*takut mati kar...*) and Hokkien (*kia si ar?*) and ends the passage with a smiling emoticon, all adding to the aural feel and comic effect of the post. The topic was whether *teh tarik* is a health threat, as recently reported in the Malaysian press:

Err … met up with a couple of seasoned forumers last night for the regular cuppa TT … as Orchi got there earlier … it was late n Orchi felt a tinch of sleepiness … so Orchi ordered a glass of kopi-o ice … which was rare thing to happen … n the mamak looked at Orchi one kind …

Then the first thing when the boyz came … one of them noticed that Orchi was drinking kopi-o ice instead … so they started firing Orchi what … 'Orchi takut mati kar ... kia si ar?' ...:) ['Orchi afraid to die?'].

To this, another poster replied in standard, emoticon-free Malaysian English but keeping the momentum of the conversation which involved other people and went on for some time (four web pages in total):

> It's the overall sugar intake combined with lack of exercise which make us obese and stoke-prone, not specifically teh tarik etc.

> And by the way, the syrup stuff that's often being served at kenduris etc is signficantly more unhealthy than teh tarikh.

What are the main characteristics of thread sociality? First, it relies on a non-deliberative, recorded, public form of discourse. Because of the narrowcast quasi-orality of thread exchanges, an interesting form of intimacy arises: a false intimacy. Although it feels as if one is sharing thoughts, experiences and emotions with an intimate group of conversational partners, one is simultaneously aware that anyone in the whole wide web could be lurking. Furthermore, unlike a public lecture or a political speech, threaded discourse is not monological but polylogical: it typically relies on three or more conversational partners for its sustenance. This explains why my own thread did not fare well. First, I had failed to draw into my thread a dynamic group of participants to build the required momentum that would 'carry' the thread forth. Moreover, I had adopted a monological, lecture-like tone in spite of my efforts at writing in conversational English.

Second, despite being web-based, threaded sociality is sequential. This is an important point to stress given the common perception that the Web is an inherently multidirectional, hypertextual milieu where users are free to create their own paths as they go along (Castells 2001). While it is true that thread participants frequently post hyperlinks to other sites, thread users of all kinds (whether they are moderators, posters or lurkers) are still constrained in their thread agency by the serial, sequential nature of this Internet technology. In contrast to the relatively messy exchanges of offline encounters, thread postings are discrete, securely bounded communicative acts. To make sense of a thread and contribute to it, participants must first gain a basic understanding of its recent history, an understanding that is easily within reach by scrolling up the thread. This micro-historical learning is aided by an automated feed that allows users to receive email alerts with links to their favourite threads each time these are reactivated: users subscribe to threads, not to the forum as a whole.

Third, although the forum's dominant sociality is web-based, some of the longer threads undergo offline phases throughout their life

courses. One of the oldest and lengthiest threads on USJ.com.my is devoted to arranging monthly *teh tarik* meetings like the one that opens
this chapter. This thread had clocked 889 posts and close to 35,000 viewings as of 3 April 2006. By 24 January 2011 the thread had 2,837 posts,
over 125,000 viewings and 190 pages![3] These sessions take place on the
first Friday of every month and attract some ten to fifteen enthusiasts. Although inseparable from the online threads, such face-to-face encounters have their own polylogical character, albeit of the offline variety: ut-
terances overlap, unmoderated topics and sub-topics break off rapidly,
and the group splinters into sub-groups. On one on the several sessions
I attended, a habitual forum poster who had arrived late was welcomed
with the greeting: 'Here comes the missing link!', a witty reference to
a faulty hyperlink he had recently posted on a thread. The conversation soon shifted to a different topic, namely the Neighbourhood Watch
scheme. It then returned to forum matters, moving on to the antics of
an unruly resident, followed by a story about the ordeal of entering the
United States in the post-9/11 era, then back to the Neighbourhood
Watch scheme, on to the question of why some races excel at certain
Olympic sports but not others, and so on until the end of the session.

Finally, in the specific case of the Subang Jaya e-Community forum,
thread sociality is marked by the conflicting priorities of the forum administrators on the one hand, and most regular users on the other. For
the management team led by the activist Jeff Ooi, at least until he became occupied with extra-local matters (see Chapter 5), the forum is
an experimental means towards an end, namely a more accountable,
efficient local government as Malaysia moves towards the Knowledge
Society. For most users, however, the forum is primarily a source of local information, entertainment and conviviality – one of Oldenburg's
(1989) 'third places', that is, venues where suburbanites can socialise
outside the home and the workplace, such as pubs, bowling clubs and
post offices. When a critical issue that affects them directly emerges on
the forum many will join the campaigning, but during peaceful periods
most will remain uninvolved. These conflicting goals are expressed in
a frequently invoked distinction between 'small talk' and 'serious talk'.
Thus in April 2006 a revealing exchange took place between the forum's main moderator, KW Chang, and a group of forum users. The
moderator had started a thread announcing that he was about to move
a number of small-talk threads to a specialist sub-forum so that the main
forum could be reserved for important community matters, as originally
intended by the portal's founding father, Jeff Ooi. A lively debate ensued in which forum users protested this plan, arguing that such a move
would condemn the chit-chat threads to a premature death, as few peo-

ple ever use the sub-forums. Moreover, they questioned the moderator's dismissal of small talk as mere *lepak* (Malay for idling or loitering), adding that small talk can sometimes lead to great things. Eventually the moderator relented and the suspect threads were spared.

How does thread sociality articulate with Subang Jaya's field of residential affairs? First, USJ.com.my's independence from the state places it firmly in the non-governmental sector of the field. But it is important, once again, not to conflate our folk and technical terms. While during calm periods the forum lives up to its name as a cordial informational market, the collective mood can change very rapidly from one of conviviality to another of confrontation and strong language, sometimes leading to collective action. At such times the forum morphs into an 'arena', as we saw in the previous chapter's Internet dramas. The reader will recall that in Turner's field theory, an arena is a 'bounded spatial unit in which precise, visible antagonists, individual or corporate, contend with one another for prizes and/or honour' (Turner 1974: 132–33). Arenas are 'explicit frames' in which 'nothing is left merely implied' and major decisions are taken in public view (1974: 134). With his arena coinage, Victor Turner was distancing himself from game theory and other rational actor models that had dominated political anthropology since the 1960s. Turner emphasised that an arena is neither a marketplace nor a forum, although they can both become an arena 'under appropriate field conditions' (1974: 134). These conditions have been met a number of times throughout USJ.com.my's decade-long history, especially when residents have confronted the local authorities over an issue of general concern, as we saw in Chapter 6.

Internal Differences

This chapter has revealed not a single homogenous 'field sociality' but rather an internally differentiated field of striving with various forms of sociality distinguished by the nature of their interactions, discourses and field articulations. Subang Jaya's residents and local authorities are not appropriating the Internet wholesale. Like people around the globe they are appropriating Internet technologies selectively, for specific purposes (Miller and Slater 2000) and within unique fields of organised striving. My analysis suggests that which Internet technologies are adopted will depend not only on their cost and technical affordances (Wellman et al. 2003) but also on the adopting field's inner differentiation (see Calhoun 1992: 38, quoted in Benson 2007: 4).

Thus, all three initiatives analysed above (Neighbourhood Watch, the JKP system and USJ.com.my) have sought to foster online discourse and conviviality through web forums, but only the latter has succeeded. This success can be attributed in part to this web portal's symbolic location at the heart of the non-governmental field sector (which has encouraged independent-minded residents to participate), and in part to the virtual lack of thematic restrictions, which gives it an edge over the Neighbourhood Watch forum with its narrow crime remit. The analysis also showed that certain field socialities are more prone than others to fluctuations in their 'moods'. Careful diachronic attention to these mood swings can teach us about a field's uneven patterns of socio-technological change and continuity, with some field niches enjoying better insulation from external pressures than others (Epstein 1958, Bourdieu 1996). By drawing on the field theoretical lexicon of both Bourdieu and the Manchester School, I was able to bring a set of concepts that lie outside the community/network paradigm (e.g., field, interaction, sociality, arena) to bear on the ethnographic analysis.

Notes

1. See http://www.thefreedictionary.com/deliberate (consulted July 2007).
2. See http://usj18.nwatch.net.my/article.cfm?id=68 (consulted August 2007).
3. By 27 August 2009 the thread had already grown to 2,707 posts, nearly 90,000 viewings and 181 pages.

Conclusion

Looking back at the history of the field of residential affairs in Subang Jaya from 1992 to 2009 (see Chronology), four calendar years stand out as having been particularly significant: 1999, 2001, 2004 and 2008.

In 1999 both continuity and change were in evidence in the field. On the one hand, Lee Hwa Beng who represented Malaysia's ruling coalition was re-elected as state assemblyman for a second term. Meanwhile three initiatives that were to have a great impact on the field were born that year, namely the federal project SJ2005, Raymond Tan's Neighbourhood Watch and Jeff Ooi's e-Community Portal (USJ.com.my).

Two major events took place in 2001. In February the municipal council, led by its ambitious president, Ahmad Fuad, created a residents' committees (JKP) system in line with the United Nation's Local Agenda 21, aimed at fostering 'good local governance' around the globe. The committees were to have their own dedicated portal, e-JKP. This was also partly a response to the ever more assertive local Internet activists, with Fuad often finding himself at the receiving end of Jeff Ooi's sharp editorials. Then in August 2001 a shockwave struck the field of residential affairs. Raymond Tan's small neighbourhood scheme had been awarded the equivalent of 300,000 US dollars as part of SJ2005, a federal project that aimed at transforming Subang Jaya into a 'smart community' by 2005. This huge influx of public monies into a small corner of the field dismayed both Fuad and Ooi who felt excluded from the partnership.

The year 2004 was one of mobilisations. In June, a small group of residents incurred the wrath of Jeff Ooi when they protested against the council bearing the USJ.com.my domain name on a banner without Jeff's authorisation. This led to a short-lived 'Internet drama' on the online forum and to the introduction of stricter posting rules. In late September, another Internet drama unfolded, only this time bringing together a formidable alliance of residents' groups led by Raymond Tan and Jeff Ooi to campaign against the council-approved building of a food court on land earmarked for a police station. The residents used various Internet and mobile technologies to coordinate their actions, claiming victory in front of the nation's television cameras on 4 October 2004. On 28 December, the Asian tsunami appeal was launched by a group of local Internet activists and endorsed by local politicians, raising a total of 25,000 ringgits (7,000 US dollars) in a few days.

Finally, in March 2008 a young opposition candidate with the Democratic Action Party (DAP) named Hannah Yeoh was elected new state assemblywoman for Subang Jaya. Lee Hwa Beng had stood for parliament but he lost the elections and retired from politics. Meanwhile, in the northern state of Penang, Jeff Ooi won a parliamentary seat also with DAP – Malaysia's first blogger to become a member of parliament.

These micro-historical milestones amount to a collection of loosely related events unless we can theorise them. In the foregoing chapters I was able to do precisely that through a synthesis of the field theories of Bourdieu and the Manchester School and a set of conceptual tools – some borrowed, others self-fashioned – that included 'Internet field', 'field of residential affairs', 'field station', 'Internet drama', 'field arena', 'residential socialities' and others. Like Eric Klinenberg (2005) in his study of American youth media, I have found field theory to be 'a useful way of seeing patterns within a messy domain of social action' (Couldry 2007: 211), in this case the domain of residential governance in Subang Jaya. Local agents operate across two main types of field site (both online and offline): regular 'stations' where the recursive practices of reproducing the field take place (e.g., online forums, mailing lists, night patrols, committee meetings, MP surgeries) and irregular 'arenas' (often those very same stations but temporarily morphed into sites of conflict) where social dramas break out and demand a resolution (Turner 1974).

In common with other fields of residential affairs (see Chapter 1), Subang Jaya's can be represented in the shape of an inverted T:⊥. The vertical axis stands for the three tiers of government (from top to bottom: federal, state and local). The horizontal axis represents the local-level actors, with residents' groups on the left, private firms on the right and the municipal council (MPSJ) in the middle, at the intersection of the two axes. Internet-savvy activists, politicians and council staff do not operate in a cyberspatial void: their practices are unavoidably shaped by their location within the inverted T of the field of residential affairs. Whatever their political affiliations, personal charisma and technical expertise, state assemblypersons such as Lee Hwa Beng and his successor Hannah Yeoh cannot but go 'down to the ground' (*turun padang*) on a regular basis in order to abide by the fundamental law of their subfield. Their Internet practices (e.g., sharing digital photographs) will serve the imperative to *turun padang* so that they will not only 'be seen' on the ground, but crucially will be seen to be resolving local issues. The proof of the *padang* is not in the eating but in the fixing. Similarly, in their heyday leading residents such as Jeff Ooi or Raymond Tan had no choice but to abide by the law of their own residential subfield: the law of selfless volunteerism. Residents who wish to make a contribution to 'the community' must freely volunteer their time and labour (including their digital labour) for the greater good, in the process earning symbolic not financial capital.

Putting now these two accounts together – the historical milestones and the inverted T of residential governance – the outline of a theory of Internet localization begins to appear. This is necessarily a parochial theory based on the empirical materials gathered in Subang Jaya. I wish nonetheless to suggest that, with some modifications, this theoretical model should find wider applicability to other localities across South East Asia and elsewhere. Let us rewind to 1999, a foundational year that saw the birth of SJ2005, Neighbourhood Watch and USJ.com.my as well as Lee Hwa Beng's consolidation as a popular state assemblyman. Observing the ⊥-shaped field we see a number of changes with respect to previous years. Where previously the top of the vertical axis was a dark spot, we now have a bright beacon of Internet hope in SJ2005 – a federally-funded local e-Governance project that should put Subang Jaya ahead of all other local authorities in the country by the year 2005. Two other bright dots are visible, both on the left foot of the ⊥. On the far end we find a proudly independent Subang Jaya e-Community Portal. It has just scored its first victory against an understaffed, barely two-years-old municipal council over a sudden rise in local taxes. Still on the left foot but closer to the council we find a less confrontational Neighbourhood Watch scheme led by local residents who are willing to work with the authorities. Meanwhile, half way up the vertical axis we find continuity: Lee Hwa Beng has retained his state-level post after having spent a great deal of time at ground level, proving his tireless commitment to his constituents.

Fast forward two years to August 2001. The ⊥-shaped field of residential affairs has seen two important changes this calendar year. First, in February the municipal council's large dot begot a smaller dot which is now placed to its left. This smaller dot is the residents' committees (JKP) system whose mission is to act as a conduit between the residents and the council. Just recently, in August, Raymond Tan's small Neighbourhood Watch scheme was awarded over one million ringgit (about 300,000 US dollars) under the SJ2005 project and is shining very brightly to the chagrin of other local Internet players on either side of the residential subfield. The two parties that feel most aggrieved are Jeff Ooi's independent Subang Jaya e-Community Portal and the council-dependent JKP system. This uneven allocation of federal funds spells the end of SJ2005, a project that relied on the cooperation of the entire field of residential affairs to create a sustainable tri-sectoral partnership built on an advanced Internet infrastructure.

We are now studying the ⊥ diagram at the end of 2004. The municipal council is shining less brightly as Fuad (later to become Kuala Lumpur's new mayor) has left his post and been replaced by a less dynamic council president. Further up the axis, SJ2005 has all but faded away. Down the far-left end of the horizontal line we can see that the Subang Jaya e-Community Portal went through a slight turmoil in June over a misused domain name (USJ.com.my), but the drama was overcome after the culprits took redressive action. In October those same activists joined forces with residents from across the left foot of the ⊥ to campaign against the municipal council over plans to build a food court on land reserved for a police station. The food court would have benefitted a number of players from the right foot of the diagram, i.e., the local private sector, as well as the municipal council. The residents achieved their aims through the deft use of a range of mobile phones and web platforms in full view of the national mass media – the most formidable alliance that the field had ever seen. It was as if the entire residential subsector of the field (the left foot) had become electrified for a short period of time. The year ended with another broad-based Internet and mobile phone campaign, this time involving not only the residents but also their state and federal representatives up the vertical axis – a local fund-raising drive on an ecumenical issue: the Indian Ocean tsunami.

Moving closer to the present day, by April 2008 the field of residential affairs looks very changed. The political earthquake that has shaken Malaysia following the considerable electoral gains of the opposition DAP has also made an impact on Subang Jaya's field of residential affairs. Half way up the vertical axis we now find a young DAP woman, Hannah Yeoh, 28, who until recently had no political experience but is now the new state assemblyperson for Subang Jaya. Not only that, she is also a popular blogger, has thousands of Facebook friends and has been interviewed on YouTube by the independent online newspaper Malaysiakini (note that neither Facebook nor YouTube existed in 2004). With Yeoh in charge, seven municipal councillors are now non-political appointments drawn from the non-governmental sector, and the residents' committees (JKP) are also changing. Meanwhile at the horizontal level of residential governance, the extreme-left outfit USJ.com.my has now an absentee landlord by the name of Jeff Ooi, another blogger turned politician, who is now a new DAP member of parliament in the far-off Jelutong seat (Penang). In Jeff's absence, the forum manager KW Chang decides to put a stop to the excessive 'politicking' on the site by closing down the more blatantly partisan threads. Raymond Tan has less time to devote to his Neighbourhood Watch activities but his spot on the residents' subfield is kept alight by a group of residents who have pioneered a new SMS alert system in cooperation with the police.

Recapitulating the Argument

In this study I have drawn from anthropological research in a Malaysian suburb to argue that Internet technologies and practices are ever more implicated in the 'production of locality' (Appadurai 1996), that is, in how local agents co-create places in which to live, work and play. I arrived at this conclusion by stepping outside the current conceptual paradigm that dominates research and discussion of Internet worlds, namely the community/network paradigm, which I defined as the ubiquitous overreliance on the entwined notions of community and network to describe and analyse such social worlds.[1] By removing these conceptual blinkers, I was able to expand the study's conceptual horizons and map a far more complex and fluid socio-political landscape. The study shows that there is no 'local community' being impacted upon that 'network of networks' known as the Internet. Eschewing the conceptual black box of 'local community', I made use of a range of more precise concepts to track the Internet practices of local agents across space and time, including 'field of residential affairs', 'station', 'arena', 'action-set', 'social drama' and 'committee'.

I defined 'the field of residential affairs' as a domain of practical endeavour and struggle in which local agents (activists, politicians, councillors, journalists and others) compete and cooperate over matters of concern to local residents, a domain increasingly mediated by Internet technologies and practices. Instead of 'community leaders' or 'opinion leaders' I adopted a practice-theoretical idiom and tracked the field's leading practitioners across two main kinds of sites: 'stations' (sites of field reproduction) and 'arenas' (sites of field change). Such sites were shown to be variously mediated by the Internet, ranging from online sites such as local web forums to predominantly offline sites such as residents' committees and neighbourhood patrols.

What can we conclude from this exploration? First, we can be confident that it is indeed possible to chronicle and theorise processes of Internet localization – processes whereby local agents appropriate certain Internet technologies and practices in order to pursue local goals –

without recourse to the community/network paradigm that dominates contemporary Internet studies (see Chapter 1). Second, local Internet fields of residential affairs are not homogenous but plural in their forms of sociality, hence my use in a previous chapter of the plural 'residential socialities'. Third, field agents, agencies, practices and technologies may come and go, but the basic design of the field of residential affairs (a vertical axis standing on a horizontal axis) remains unaltered. New media theorists and Internet activists may dream of 'flattened hierarchies', 'self-organising systems' or 'flexible networks' but to date these ideas have had no effect on the hierarchical structure of the modern state, built on several tiers of government and administration. To return to Miller and Slater's (2000) point about people around the world not appropriating the Internet wholesale but rather selectively – thereby making it 'their' Internet – with residential governance this must be qualified by saying that this process is strongly shaped by the resilient structures of the modern state. Local activists, politicians and journalists in Subang Jaya have indeed found innovative ways of pursuing their own aims through an ensemble of Internet and mobile technologies, but their practices have not altered one iota the hierarchical structure of the modern polity in which they are embedded.

I have resisted the urge to make epochal claims based on my research (see Chapter 2). Subang Jaya is a cutting-edge Internet laboratory and there are intriguing comparative questions emerging from this Malaysian case study, particularly with regard to analogous processes of Internet localization and forms of 'banal activism' in other residential suburbs around the globe. Yet pointing at similarities across locales is quite different from claiming that the events I chronicle here usher in a new era of Digital Democracy, a Knowledge Society or some such capitalised shorthand.

Like Miller and Slater (2000) in their Trinidad ethnography, I have investigated a diverse range of Internet-related practices in a non-Western country. However, there is a fundamental difference here of geopolitical scale: the present study concerns itself with 'the local' in the strict sense of this term. That is, it works at the municipal, not national, level of governance, activism and sociality. This is an important point to stress, for in contemporary social and cultural theory we often find the terms 'local' and 'global' paired together, with the former usually standing in for the nation-state. Moreover, as mentioned in Chapter 2, scholars in South East Asia and other regions who have discussed the Internet's democratising potential have to date concentrated on the national level of governance but largely ignored the local level. Going against the grain of influential social theories that see digitally-mediated activism moving away from 'geographical issues of place' and towards translocal 'identity politics' (Loader 2008: 1928; see also Castells 2007), the present study shows that local activism merits at least as much attention as other forms of activism.

Further Research

The theoretical and empirical findings presented in this book suggest a number of avenues for future comparative research. For the sake of brevity I will discuss these avenues in relation to three specialist fields of particular relevance to this case study: suburban studies, legal and political anthropology and Internet studies.

From a suburban studies perspective, there is the fascinating comparative question of 'why Subang Jaya?' Why is there such a thriving Internet activism scene in this particular suburb at this particular time? Is this a unique case or are there similar suburban exemplars elsewhere? This is in fact a question that Internet innovators in the suburb have often asked themselves. Although I have no conclusive answer at this point in time, five key ingredients make Subang Jaya stand out. First, Subang Jaya (and especially its USJ district) has a majority of middle- and upper-middle income residents who came to this award-winning township in search of the Malaysian dream, a dream of sustained growth, family-building and social mobility. Yet soon they saw that dream dissipate following the 1997 financial crash and subsequent political crisis, along with deteriorating local conditions in the suburb (traffic congestion, scarce school places, rising crime, etc.). Second, Subang Jaya and USJ hold a large population tightly compressed into a small territory. This not only put pressure on services regarded as essential by upwardly mobile settlers, but also provided a vast pool of disgruntled residents from which a coterie of motivated grassroots leaders emerged. Third, by far the greater proportion of the township's middle-class majority is made up of ethnic Chinese Malaysians who are (self-) employed in the private sector; that is, people who are generally enterprising but much more vulnerable than the state-sponsored Malay middle class to an economic downturn and a deteriorating suburb (Chapter 3). Fourth, local governance in Malaysia has suffered from a glaring democratic deficit ever since local government elections were suspended in the 1960s. This has resulted in Chinese-majority areas such as Subang Jaya having unelected local councils staffed almost entirely by Malays. Although few Subang Jaya residents have joined calls for a return of local elections, this deficit has fostered the growth of banal (cyber)activism – a species of activism centred on non-racial issues such as crime, infrastructure and waste disposal. Finally, Subang Jaya is blessed with an impressive number of 'technopreneurs' who work in the region's strong technological sector and combine political acumen with digital skills (as well as an unflagging faith in technological progress). These individuals are keen to make their mark on the locality and willing to devote time and effort to this end. Together, all five ingredients add to a potent mix that is unlikely to be found in quite that strength in many other locales around the globe.

Nevertheless, this study paves the way for future comparisons of 'natural experiments' (Diamond and Robinson 2010) with Internet localization in other suburbs, both in South East Asia and beyond. To illustrate this comparative potential, let us take a recent study of media and activism in an upmarket housing estate near Melbourne known by the pseudonym of 'Kookaburra Hollow' (Arnold et al. 2007).

Like their Subang Jaya counterparts, Kookaburra Hollow incomers arrived in pursuit of the dream of a green, safe and hi-tech suburbia away from the chaos and pollution of urban life. They too, however, soon found that all was not well in their leafy neighbourhood. As part of an attractive package, the developers had offered prospective buyers hi-speed broadband connections in every household. Alas this failed to materialise in many homes, which triggered the onset of Kookaburra's own brand of banal activism aimed at securing this technology. Other complaints centred on allegations of poorly built houses and a scarcity of public amenities. Residents turned to the local intranet facility – originally envisaged by the developers as a site for convivial community-building – to plan and carry out their campaign, along with face-to-face meetings and homemade banners. The fledgling intranet station morphed into a field arena where the two camps clashed as a local social drama unfolded. Representing the developers was Bill Flanders (also known as 'Big Brother') who was the intranet forum moderator. Opposing him stood the controversial figure of Anthony Briggs, a vocal resident regarded by some neighbours as being too confrontational. The drama escaped the control of local actors when a popular current-affairs programme on television ran a segment on the conflict at the request of leading residents. Following the airing of this show, a 'growing chorus' of residents expressed their concern that the media coverage might undermine property values at Kookaburra Hollow.

As this succinct account of the drama shows, Kookaburra's field of residential affairs is divided into two main subfields or sectors: a private sector (the developers) and a residents' sector. The authors describe the arrangement as one of 'privatised governance' in which most of the functions that one would normally associate with a local council are devolved to a private firm (see Low 2003). As in Subang Jaya, there is a strong rhetoric of community, solidarity and rootedness at work across this divide. What I earlier termed 'an interest in disinterestedness' (Bourdieu 1996), Arnold and his co-authors (2007:10) label 'interested solidarity'. That is to say, residents constantly remind one another that it is in their self-interest to throw in their lot with the rest of 'the community'. Yet just as in the early days of banal activism in Subang Jaya, Kookaburra residents soon learned that involving the mass media in a local dispute can be a double-edged sword.

One area of great comparative potential is the question of personal media and suburban leadership (Chapter 5). The following working assumptions could be tested in Kookaburra Hollow and other middle-class suburbs (see Durington 2007, Hampton 2003, Hampton and Wellman 2003, Mesch and Levanon 2003). First, we can anticipate that councillors, politicians and leading residents will use personal media for banal activism in conjunction with collective media (e.g., mailing lists, web forums, intranets, group blogs, Facebook groups) and, less frequently, mass media. This form of activism springs from the universal middle-class imperative to collectively create and maintain a local environment conducive to family-building. As the old proverb goes, 'It takes a whole village to raise a child'. Both established and aspiring local leaders will put their personal media to work for the communitarian interest in disinterestedness (or interested solidarity) that characterises suburban fields of residential affairs. Second, local leaders can be regarded as leading practitioners within the field of residential affairs; that is, practitioners who are skilled at putting their social ties, personal media and other resources to work both within the field's regular stations (residents' committees, MP surgeries, town hall meetings, web forum threads, Twitter hashtags) as well as its more volatile arenas – those sites in which the field's contradictions and underlying tensions will at times surface in a dynamic assemblage of people, issues and technologies. Third, all personal media practices, including those of local leaders, are shaped by the vagaries of the life course and collective history. Some field positions, however, are more prone to conflict and turbulence than others, particularly those in which a leader must reconcile the conflicting logics of the vertical and horizontal subfields – for example, a leading resident who is both a community activist and the loyal client of a political candidate.

A second avenue for further research opens at the intersection between media anthropology and legal-political anthropology. The East African work of the American legal anthropologist Sally Falk Moore (2000, 2005) is especially pertinent here.[2] In a piece originally published in 1973, Falk Moore argues that legal scholars have tended to overemphasise state laws at the expense of 'spontaneous' rules emerging out of social life, adding that modern individuals' relations with the body politic are mediated by the various social fields in which they operate (2000: 56, 80). For their part, social anthropologists such as Fredrik Barth (1966) and other 1960s transactionalists focused on norms arising within a given field but neglected to examine how state laws impinge on fields that already have customs and rules.

Falk Moore argues that the social fields typically studied by anthropologists are 'semi-autonomous': they can generate customs, rules and symbols internally but are 'vulnerable to rules and decisions and other forces' originating in the wider world (2000: 55). Understanding the processes whereby endogenous rules become effective should be of interest to law-makers, as these are the very processes that will often determine whether or not state-made legal rules are eventually adopted into a given social field (2000: 57). Falk Moore coined the concept of 'semi-autonomous social field' to reveal the links between 'the internal workings of an observable social field and its points of articulation with a larger setting' (2000: 78). To understand social fields, she argues, we must examine how they articulate with one another, for in complex societies fields are invariably entangled in webs of interdependence (2000: 57–58).

Whilst modern legislation is increasingly designed to bring about social change, new laws often result in unintended consequences (2000: 58). A great deal of legislation, says Falk Moore, is piecemeal and it is adopted into fields unevenly. 'A court of legislature can make custom law. A semi-autonomous social field can make law its custom' (2000: 79). Field agents can mobilise or threaten to mobilise external forces in their dealings with one another – but legal rules are only a small part of the whole picture. Often participants will comply with the rules of the field (legal, non-legal and illegal) so as to be able to derive financial or other rewards from their participation (2000: 64). Even though semi-autonomous fields will vary greatly in their lifespan, extent of conscious design, top-down or bottom-up nature and so on, most fields will exhibit some form of resistance to external pressure (2000: 81). For example, among the Chagga people of Mount Kilimanjaro where Falk Moore conducted extended fieldwork, the resilience of the indigenous 'lineage-neighbourhood complex' in the face of Tanzania's state socialism suggests that semi-autonomous fields will tend to resist any curtailing of their autonomy.

Falk Moore's discussion of semi-autonomous social fields resonates strongly with the theoretical model developed in the present study, built around the concept of field of residential affairs. It also suggests the need for future studies of Internet localization that bring into the analysis insights from legal and political anthropology. Take the second Internet drama analysed in Chapter 6, in which I noted how local activists in Subang Jaya and elsewhere seek to identify 'procedural lapses' in projects they object to, so that 'the project can be challenged in the administrative court and any further planning or development works suspended' (Newman 1994: 220, quoted in Abram 1998: 13). One key question for future local Internet studies is the part played by Internet technologies and practices in the dynamic set of legal, non-legal and illegal rules found within a given field of residential affairs. (Of course, precisely what counts as being 'illegal' is likely to be at the heart of many disputes between the local residents and the authorities.)

A third comparative avenue opened by *Localizing the Internet* is the use of an expanded conceptual lexicon to investigate Internet-related place-making and residential sociality outside the community/network paradigm. Like Boellstorff in his ethnography of the virtual world Second Life (2008), in this book I have explored the relationship between Internet technologies and place-making (see also Green et al. 2005) – and more specifically, the production of locality. The difference is that whilst Second Life is primarily an online place with offline ramifications, Subang Jaya is first and foremost an offline place with online extensions. This contrast makes the similarities between the perennial concerns of Second Life and Subang Jaya residents (e.g., with crime, property, cooperation and sociality) truly striking. Boellstorff's insistence that Second Life is a place echoes Rheingold's (1993) argument about the Well, a pioneering 'virtual community' built in the San Francisco Bay area. For Rheingold, the Well was a virtual – albeit text-based – 'third place' in Oldenburg's (1989) sense of the term, i.e., a place of suburban conviviality that is neither the home nor the workplace. Both studies raise fascinating questions for anthropologists working on internet issues about what constitutes an online place, particularly in view of the current rethinking of notions such as 'place' and 'space' in anthropology and neighbouring fields.[3] These are intriguing issues that I could not pursue in this study but that call for further interdisciplinary research.

Notes

1. Two recent examples of this dependence on community and network include the Debating Communities and Networks Conference organised by students from Curtin University and Open Universities Australia in 2010 (http://network-conference.netstudies.org/) and chapter 4 of Nancy Baym's new book, *Personal Connections in the Digital Age* (2010), entitled 'Communities and Networks'. Many more examples could be given of this enduring conceptual marriage.

2. I am grateful to two anonymous readers for stressing this study's legal-political anthropology dimensions, and to one of them for the Falk Moore (2000) reference.

3. See, for instance, Casey (2001), Ingold (2008), Massey (2005), Pink (2009) and Thrift (2006).

FAQs

In keeping with the subject-matter of *Localizing the Internet*, it is appropriate to end with that most characteristic of web genres: the FAQs (Frequently Asked Questions). This book has been in the making for seven years, and integral to this process have been the many conferences and seminars at which I have presented work in progress related to this project. Below I provide a small sample of the many questions that people have asked me over the years.[1]

Q. What sort of 'community' are we talking about here? What are its online/offline dimensions, affects, etc?

In this project I have tried to steer clear of the notion of 'community' as a sociological or anthropological concept as I find it to be a normative ideal that lacks a precise empirical referent and is therefore unresearchable as an actual social formation (see Chapter 2). 'Community' is a useful fiction that people in many places use for public rhetoric (Amit and Rapport 2002), but in my view it is not a sharp sociological tool. In *Localizing the Internet* I explore how settlers of a suburban frontier appropriate various Internet technologies to create sets of social relations that did not exist before, thereby 'producing locality' (Appadurai 1996). I have gradually come to realise that we need to distinguish between social life forms that are amenable to empirical investigation (e.g., residents' committees, mosques, action-sets, personal networks, Google groups, Twitter tribes) and those that are transempirical and therefore unresearchable (e.g., communities, nations, Heaven, Hell). Yes, you can certainly document how people feel about 'their community' but always bearing in mind that communities are heart-warming ideals, not empirical actualities. They have feelings towards an imaginary entity.

Q. What difference does it actually make to posit the existence of social fields instead of communities? Are you not still talking about the same thing using a different term?

No, although invisible, social fields are not figments of the imagination; they are not normative ideals unmoored from social actualities – this is what distinguishes them from communities. Fields are domains of practice in which variously positioned agents bring to the field's 'games' (Bourdieu) differing amounts and kinds of capital, competing and co-operating over the rewards offered by that field (financial, symbolic, social, etc.). It is not my intention to propose the notion of social field as an ersatz for 'community'. What I advocate is the broadening out of the new media studies lexicon from its current fixation with two or three keywords (community, network, public sphere).

Q. What can you tell us about the constitutive role of conflicts in emerging forms of residential sociality, including when conflict creates an internal solidarity or a feeling of community?

Indeed, one of the turning points in the history of internet activism in Subang Jaya was when in 1999 leading residents harnessed various digital technologies available at the time (email, newsgroups, databases) to successfully campaign against a sharp increase in local taxation. So yes, conflicts are more than simply disruptions to the regular cycle of activities of peacetime politics (as perhaps implied by my discussion of personal media and local leadership, in Chapter 5); they can also be constitutive of new residential socialities and practices.

Q. You talk about local leaders and their personal media but how do ordinary residents use such media?

In Chapter 5 I focused on local leaders because I wanted to argue that despite their deft use of a range of personal media (email, blogs, PDAs, digital cameras, mobiles, Facebook, etc.) they are never above the laws of the fields in which they operate. In the field of residential affairs, lo-cal leaders cannot but surrender their personal media practices to the collectivist ethos and communitarian media rhetoric or face the conse-quences. By contrast, political blogging affords exceptional individuals such as Jeff Ooi (one of the pioneering Internet activists in Subang Jaya who went on to become a political blogger and a Member of Parlia-ment) much more autonomy and 'networked individualism' (Wellman) than the relentlessly sociocentric 'community media'. The online scene in Subang Jaya is dominated by a small number of sites, especially by the hugely active Subang Jaya e-Community Portal (USJ.com.my) which has been going strong for ten years and boasts thousands upon thousands of threads. These threads can be started and extended by any subscriber, and there are over thirty thousand forum subscribers, so it is very much an environment open to 'ordinary residents'. That said, as I have stressed in Chapter 2, this is not a 'digital divide' study but rather a study based on having 'followed the action' in a largely middle-class suburb. There are undoubtedly exclusions at work in the field of residential affairs (e.g., the poor, foreign immigrants, non-English speakers, etc.) but these mechanisms are beyond the scope of the present study.

Q. Surely this whole study is about the elite? What has this got to do with the majority of the population who are just ordinary people?

No, I think it is crucial that we distinguish between the elites and the middle classes. As I argued in Chapter 3, most Subang Jaya residents are middle-class, not members of Malaysia's ruling elite. Their concerns and demands are very much those of people who are neither rich nor poor and are intent on reproducing their families' cultural and economic capital. Living in an underserviced, overcrowded suburban frontier and in an uncertain political and economic climate, many parents in Subang Jaya are finding it difficult to attain their goals – for instance, to give their children 'a good education'.

Q. What difference do Internet and other digital technologies actually make to local power relations? Would the demonstration against the local authorities over the building of a food court [Chapter 6] have happened without these technologies?

We shall never know for certain as the Internet and other technologies are inseparable from the rest of what goes on in Subang Jaya and similar localities, but that demonstration was a good example of how local activists mobilised a range of digital technologies (email, mailing lists, web forums, blogs, texting, etc.) to mount a campaign very quickly and get the authorities to change their mind on an issue. For instance, elected politicians were texted and asked to state publicly where they stood on the unresolved dispute, and their responses were relayed back to the general population via the web.

Q. You have conducted fieldwork among the Iban of Borneo [Postill 2006]. How do you think the new digital technologies may be affecting Iban leadership in the longhouses?

A very good question. I wish I knew! My guess is that the basic governance template and implications of the new digital technologies are very similar in both settings, i.e., the field of residential affairs in which a longhouse is embedded also has a horizontal axis marked by its egalitarianism and communitarianism as well as a vertical axis/subfield that goes up from the headman to the native chief to the district officer and all the way up to the federal government in Peninsular Malaysia. Field agents occupying positions close to where the two axes meet (e.g., longhouse headmen) can find themselves in an awkward situation when their commitment to the longhouse 'community' (i.e., the base of the governance⊥, see Conclusion) is questioned – and this may well be happening nowadays via Internet and especially mobile technologies. One development worthy of research is the rapid growth in recent months (2009) of an Iban/Dayak blogosphere in Sarawak and its likely articulations with mobile technologies.

Q. What are the prospects for a bottom-up global movement connecting these kinds of local Internet initiatives?

The middle-aged, suburban, highly localized 'banal activism' that I describe in the book – around issues such as traffic congestion, waste disposal, and crime – is not the activism of, say, the Barcelona-based young urban transnational activists studied by Juris (2008) in *Networking Futures* or that of activists fighting to end Israel's blockade of Gaza as I write these lines in June 2010; nor is it the activism of the urban intelligentsia in Kuala Lumpur. It has its own logic, and I do not see how it can change into something else. I think it is highly unlikely that the field of residential affairs will somehow morph into the field of translocal affairs. For example, attempts at harnessing Subang Jaya's Internet activism for the nationwide campaign to bring back local elections have had no success (Chapter 4).

Q. Could you say a bit more about the interdependence of the local, state and national levels of governance? After all, you said that [the state assemblyman] Lee Hwa Beng was voted out of office in 2008 despite having done a lot for the township and being very popular with the grassroots.

All three levels are interdependent and for the first time since independence Malaysia's ruling coalition lost its absolute majority in the 2008 general elections. The answer is: I do not know why Lee did not win the parliamentary seat he contested (note that on this occasion he decided to contest at the national not state level). I have had some email reports on this but I hope to be able to follow it up on the ground in future visits to Subang Jaya.

For future updates on these issues, see my research blog, media/anthropology (http://johnpostill.wordpress.com).

Notes

1. Special thanks to colleagues and students at the Department of Sociology II, University of the Basque Country, and the Department of Southeast Asian Studies, University of Passau.

References

Abbott, J.P. 2001. 'Democracy@internet.asia? The Challenges to the Emancipatory Potential of the Net: Lessons from China and Malaysia', *Third World Quarterly* 22(1): 99–114.

——— 2004. 'The Internet, Reformasi and Democratisation in Malaysia' in E.T. Gomez (ed.) *The State of Malaysia: Ethnicity, Equity and Reform*, 79–104. London and New York: Routledge.

Abram, S. 1998. 'Introduction' in S. Abram and J. Waldren (eds) *Anthropological Perspectives on Local Development*, 1–17. London and New York: Routledge.

——— and R. Cowell. 2002. 'Lessons from Community Planning in Norway and Scotland', URL (consulted June 2010): http://www.shef.ac.uk/communityplanning/.

Agar, J., S. Green and P. Harvey. 2002. 'Cotton to Computers: from Industrial to Information Revolutions' in S. Woolgar (ed.) *Virtual Society: Technology, Cyberbole, Reality*, 264–85. Oxford: Oxford University Press.

Almeida, C. 2004. 'The homework debate: not more than two hours a day: experts', *Malay Mail Online*, 6 August 2004, http://www.emedia.com.my/Current_News/MM/Saturday/National/20040731095931. Consulted 6 August 2004.

Amit, V. 2002a. 'Anthropology and Community: Some Opening Notes' in V. Amit and N. Rapport *The Trouble with Community*, 13–25. London: Pluto.

——— 2002b. 'Reconceptualizing Community' in V. Amit (ed.) *Realizing Community: Concepts, Social Relationships and Sentiments*, 1–20. London: Routledge.

——— 2007. 'Globalization through "Weak Ties": A Study of Transnational Networks Among Mobile Professionals' in V. Amit (ed.) *Going First Class? New Approaches to Privileged Travel and Movement*, 53–71. Oxford and New York: Berghahn Books.

——— and N. Rapport. 2002. *The Trouble with Community*. London: Pluto.

Anderson, B. 1991 [1983]. *Imagined Communities: Reflections on the Origin and Spread of Nationalism*, 2nd edn. London: Verso.

Appadurai, A. 1986. 'Introduction: Commodities and the Politics of Value' in A.

Appadurai (ed.) *The Social Life of Things: Commodities in Cultural Perspective*, Cambridge: Cambridge University Press.

———1996. 'The Production of Locality'. In A. Appadurai *Modernity at Large*. Minneapolis: University of Minnesota Press.

Arnold, M., C. Shepherd and M. Gibbs. 2008. 'Trouble at Kookaburra Hollow: How Media Mediate'. *The Journal of Community Informatics* 3: 4. URL (consulted June 2010): http://www.ci-journal.net/index.php/ciej/article/view/329/380.

Aufderheide, Pat. 1995. 'The Video in the Villages Project: Videomaking with and by Brazilian Indians'. *Visual Anthropology Review* 11(2): 82–93.

Barber, K. (ed.). 2006. *Africa's Hidden Histories: Everyday Literacy and Making the Self.* Bloomington, Indiana University Press.

Barendregt, Bart and Raul Pertierra. 2008. 'Supernatural Communication in the Philippines and Indonesia'. *Handbook of Mobile Communication Studies*, 377–88. Cambridge, MA: MIT Press.

Barth, F. 1966. *Models of Social Organization.* London, Royal Anthropological Institute.

Barton, D., and K. Tusting (eds). 2005. *Beyond Communities of Practice: Language, Power and Social Context.* Cambridge: Cambridge University Press.

Begum, F. 2000. 'Cashless transactions from home or office within two years'. *The Star Online*, 24 May 2000, http://www.thestar.com.my/news/storyx1000.asp?file=/20 00/5/24/nation/2401fbha&sec. Consulted 28 July 2004.

Benson, R. 2007. 'After Habermas: The Revival of a Macro-sociology of Media'. Paper presented at the American Sociological Association Annual Conference, New York, 11 August 2007, URL (consulted December 2007): http://steinhardt.nyu. edu/scmsAdmin/uploads/000/671/Benson_ASA.pdf.

Bernama. 2003. 'Govt The Victim Of Corrupt, Inefficient Local Councils, Says Mahathir'. 27 October 2003. http://www.bernama.com/bernama/v3/p...le.php?id=26123. Consulted 21 July 2004.

Bernard, H. Russell. 1974. 'Scientists and Policy Makers: An Ethnography of Communication'. *Human Organization* 33(3): 261–75.

Bilu, Yoram and Eyal Ben-Ari. 1992. 'The Making of Modern Saints: Manufactured Charisma and the Abu-Hatseiras of Israel'. *American Ethnologist* 19(4): 672–87.

Bob, Clifford. 2005. *The Marketing of Rebellion: Insurgents, Media, and International Activism.* Cambridge: Cambridge University Press.

Boellstorff, T. 2008. *Coming of Age in Second Life: An Anthropologist Explores the Virtually Human.* Princeton: Princeton University Press.

Bourdieu, P. 1991 'The peculiar history of scientific reason', *Sociological Forum* 6(1): 3–26.

———1993. *The Field of Cultural Production.* Cambridge: Polity Press.

———1996. *The Rules of Art: Genesis and Structure of the Literary Field.* Cambridge: Polity Press.

———1998. *Practical Reason.* Cambridge: Polity Press.

Bräuchler, B. 2005. *Cyberidentities at War: Der Molukkenkonflikt im Internet.* Bielefeld: transcript.

———— and J. Postill (eds). 2010. *Theorising Media and Practice*. Oxford and New York: Berghahn Books.

Cameron, D. 2006. 'The rocket in your pocket: How mobile phones became *The Media* by stealth'. Proceedings of the 2nd joint JEANZ-JEA conference, Auckland, New Zealand, 4–6 December 2006. http://artsweb.aut.ac.nz/journalism_conference/.

Casey, E. 2001. 'Between geography and philosophy: what does it mean to be in the place-world?' *Annals of the Association of American Geographers*, Vol. 91, 683–93.

Castells, M. 2001. *The Internet Galaxy*. Oxford: Oxford University Press.

———— 2007. 'Communication, Power and Counter-Power in the Network Society'. *International Journal of Communication* 1(1): 238–66.

Chadwick, A. 2006. *Internet Politics: States, Citizens, and New Communication Technologies*. Oxford: Oxford University Press.

Chandran, P. 2003. Unpublished background paper to the 'Forum on Good Local Governance: Is it time to bring back local elections?' 3K Complex, Subang Jaya, 14 September 2003.

Chigona, W. 2006. 'Should Communal Computing Facilities Cohabit with Public Facilities?' *The Journal of Community Informatics* (2) 3, URL (consulted August 2007): http://ci-journal.net/index.php/ciej/issue/view/15.

Coleman, S. 2005. 'From The Ground Up: an evaluation of community-focused approaches to e-democracy', London, Office of the Deputy Prime Minister. www.bristol.gov.uk/ccm/cms-service/download/asset/?asset_id=27704058

Connell, R.W. 1983. *Which Way is Up?* Sydney: George Allen and Unwin Australia.

Couldry, N. 2003. 'Media Meta-capital: Extending the Range of Bourdieu's Field Theory', *Theory and Society* 32(5–6): 653–77.

———— 2004. 'Theorising Media as Practice', *Social Semiotics* 14(2): 115–32.

———— 2007 'Bourdieu and the Media: The Promise and Limits of Field Theory (Review of Benson and Neveu, 2005)', *Theory and Society* 36(2): 209–13.

Crewe , E. 2005. *Lords of Parliament: Manners, Rituals And Politics*. Manchester: Manchester University Press.

Dahlberg, L. 2001. 'Extending the Public Sphere through Cyberspace: The Case of Minnesota E-Democracy', *First Monday* 6(3), URL (consulted March 2006): http://www.firstmonday.dk/issues/issue6_3/dahlberg/.

———— 2005 'The Corporate Takeover of the Online Public Sphere: A Critical Examination, with Reference to "the New Zealand Case"', *Pacific Journalism Review* 11(1): 90–112.

Dal Fiore, F. and G. Martinotti. 2005. 'Communities vs. Networks, as the Extremes of a Continuum of Social Containers for Innovation'. Workshop proposal to 2nd International Conference on Communities and Technologies, Milan, 13–16 June 2005, URL (consulted March 2006): http://www.cct2005.disco.unimib.it/Workshop-G.htm.

Davies, W. 2004. 'Delivering ICT in Local Communities', URL (consulted March 2006): http://www.egovmonitor.com/features/wdavies.html.

———— and J. Crabtree. 2004. 'Invisible Villages: Technolocalism and Community Renewal', *Renewal* 12(1).

Day, P. 2001. *The Networked Community: Policies for a Participative Information Society*. Brighton: University of Brighton.

———— 2005. 'Sustainable Community Technology: The Symbiosis between Community Technology and Community Research', *Journal of Community Informatics* 1(3), URL (consulted June 2010): http://www.ci-journal.net/index. php/ciej/article/view/217.

Diamond, J. and J.A. Robinson (eds). 2010. *Natural Experiments of History*. Cambridge, MA: Harvard University Press.

Dickey, S. 1993. 'Politics of Adulation: Cinema and the Production of Politicians in South India'. *Journal of Asian Studies* 52(2): 340–72.

Downey, G. 2008. Review of *Mobile Communication and Society: A Global Perspective* by Manuel Castells, Mireia Fernández-Ardèvol, Jack Linchuan Qiu and Araba Sey. Cambridge, MA: MIT Press, 2006, *Technology and Culture* 49(2), April 2008.

Durington, M. 2007. 'Moral Panics in Suburban Texas'. Paper to the EASA Media Anthropology Network e-Seminar, 27 February – 6 March 2007, URL (consulted June 2010): http://www.media-anthropology.net/durington_panics.pdf.

Dutta-Bergman, M.J. 2005. 'Access to the Internet in the Context of Community Participation and Community Satisfaction', *New Media and Society* 7(1): 89–109.

Dyck, N. 2002. '"Have you been to Hayward Field?": Children's sport and the construction of community in suburban Canada' in V. Amit, *Realizing Community. Concepts, Social Relationships and Sentiments*. London: Routledge.

Edelman, M. 2005. 'When Networks Don't Work: The Rise and Fall and Rise of Civil Society Initiatives in Central America' 29–45, in *Social Movements: An Anthropological Reader*, June Nash (ed.). London: Blackwell.

Epstein, A.L. 1958. *Politics in an Urban African Community*. Manchester: Manchester University Press.

Eriksen, T.H. and F.S. Nielsen. 2001. *A History of Anthropology*. London: Pluto Press.

Evens, T.M.S. and D. Handelman (eds). 2006. *The Manchester School: Practice and Ethnographic Praxis in Anthropology*. Oxford: Berghahn Books.

Eyerman, R. 2008. *The Assassination of Theo van Gogh: From Social Drama to Cultural Trauma*. Durham, NC: Duke University Press.

Falk Moore, S. 1978. 'Law and Social Change: the Semi-autonomous Social Field as an Appropriate Subject of Study' in *Law as Process: An Anthropological Approach*. London: Routledge.

———— 2006. 'From Tribes and Traditions to Composites and Conjunctures' in T.M.S. Evens and D. Handelman (eds) *The Manchester School: Practice and Ethnographic Praxis in Anthropology*. Oxford: Berghahn Books.

Ferlander, S. and D. Timms. 2001. 'Local Nets and Social Capital', *Telematics and Informatics* 18: 51–65.

Foth, M. 2004a. 'Establishing Social Ownership in a Residential Community

Network'. Paper presented at the Building & Bridging Community Networks Conference, Brighton, 31 March – 2 April 2004, URL (consulted March 2006): http://gsb.haifa.ac.il/~sheizaf/AOIR5/140.html.

——— 2004b. 'Working Towards Continuity in a Highly Volatile Community Network'. Paper presented at the 5th Annual Conference of the Association of Internet Researchers (aoir.org), University of Sussex, Brighton, 19–22 September 2004, URL (consulted August 2007): http://eprints.qut.edu.au/archive/00001905/01/foth_aoir50.pdf.

Freeman, L. 2007. 'The study of social networks', URL (consulted August 2007): http://www.insna.org/INSNA/na_inf.html.

Gan, S., J. Gomez and J. Uwe (eds). 2004. *Asian Cyberactivism: Freedom of Expression and Media Censorship.* Bangkok: Friedrich Naumann Foundation.

Gee, J. 2005. 'Semiotic Social Spaces and Affinity Spaces' in D. Barton and K. Tusting (eds) *Beyond Communities of Practice.* Cambridge: Cambridge University Press.

Geertz, C. 1988. *Works and Lives: The Anthropologist as Author.* Stanford: Stanford University Press.

Gell, A. 1986. 'Newcomers to the Worlds of Goods: Consumption among the Muria Gonds' in A. Appadurai (ed.) *The Social Life of Things: Commodities in Cultural Perspective.* Cambridge: Cambridge University Press.

George, C. 2003. 'The Internet and the Narrow Tailoring Dilemma for "Asian" democracies', *Communication Review* 6(3): 247–68.

——— 2007. 'Media in Malaysia: Zone of Contention', *Democratization* 14(5): 893–910.

Giddens, A. 1984. *The Constitution of Society.* Cambridge: Polity.

Gledhill, J. 2000. *Power and its Disguises: Anthropological Perspectives on Politics.* London: Pluto.

Goh, B.L. 2002. *Non-Compliance: A Neglected Agenda in Urban Governance,* Johore Bahru: ISI.

Gomez, E.T. and K.S. Jomo. 1997. *Malaysia's Political Economy: Politics, Patronage and Profits.* Melbourne: Cambridge University Press.

Goody, J. 1987. *The Interface between the Written and the Oral.* Cambridge: Cambridge University Press.

Graham, G. 2005. 'Community Networking as Radical Practice', *Journal of Community Informatics* 1(3), URL (consulted August 2007): http://ci-journal.net/index.php/ciej/article/view/245.

Granovetter, M. 1973. 'The strength of weak ties', *American Journal of Sociology* 78(6): 1360–80.

Green, S., P. Harvey and H. Knox. 2005. 'Scales of Place and Networks: an Ethnography of the Imperative to Connect through Information and Communications Technologies', *Current Anthropology* 46(5): 805–26.

Guest, A. 2000. 'The mediated community', *Urban Affairs Review* 35: 603–27.

Gurstein, M. 2004. 'Editorial: Welcome to the Journal of Community Informatics', *Journal of Community Informatics* 1(1), URL (consulted March 2006): http://

www.ci-journal.net/viewarticle.php?id=29&layout=html.

———, M.J. Menou and S. Stafeev (eds) 2003. *Community Networking and Community Informatics: Prospects, Approaches, Instruments.* St Petersburg: Centre of Community Networking and Information Policy Studies (CCNS).

Hachigian, N. 2002. 'The Internet and Power in One-Party East Asian States', *Washington Quarterly* 25(3): 41–58.

Hakken, D. 1999. *Cyborgs@Cyberspace: An Ethnographer Looks to the Future.* London: Routledge.

Hampton, K.N. 2003. 'Grieving for a Lost Network: Collective Action in a Wired Suburb', *The Information Society* 19: 417–28.

——— and B. Wellman. 2003. 'Neighboring in Netville: How the Internet Supports Community and Social Capital in a Wired Suburb', *City and Community* 2(3): 277–311.

Hannerz, U. 1980. *Exploring the City: Inquiries Toward an Urban Anthropology.* New York: Columbia University.

Harper, R. 2003. 'Are mobiles good for society?' in K. Nyiri (ed.) *Mobile Democracy: Essays on Society, Self and Politics*, Passagen Verlag, Vienna, 185–214.

Haythornthwaite, C. 1998. 'A Social Network Study of the Growth of Community Among Distance Learners', *Information Research*, 4(1).

Hesmondhalgh, D. and J. Toynbee. 2006. 'A successful conference on media change and social theory', *CRESC News*, 4 December 2006, URL (consulted August 2007): http://www.cresc.ac.uk/publications/newsletters.html.

Hill, D. and K. Sen. 2000. 'The Internet in Indonesia's New Democracy' in P. Ferdinand (ed.) *The Internet, Democracy and Democratization*, 119–36. London: Frank Cass.

Hine, C. 2000. *Virtual Ethnography.* London: Sage.

Hinkelbein, O. 2008. 'Strategien zur Digitalen Integration von Migranten: Ethnographische Fallstudien in Esslingen und Hannover'. Unpublished Ph.D. thesis, University of Bremen.

Hogan, B. 2009. 'From Each According to Media? Testing Wellman's Theory of Networked Individualism'. URL (consulted June 2010): http://papers.ssrn.com/sol3/papers.cfm?abstract_id=1331009.

Holmes, L. and M. Grieco. 2001. 'The Internet, Email, and the Malaysian Political Crisis: the Power of Transparency', *Asia Pacific Business Review* 8(2): 59–72.

Horst, H. 2008. Review of Manuel Castells, Mireira Fernández-Ardèvol, Jack Linchuan Qiu and Araba Sey (eds) *Mobile Communication and Society: A Global Perspective 2006.* Cambridge, MA: MIT Press. URL (consulted June 2010): http://ironforge.hri.uci.edu/eedmlstudio/index.php/Firda_08/comments/book_review_of_mobile_communication_and_society_castells_fernandez_ardevol_/.

——— and D. Miller. 2006. *The Cell Phone: An Anthropology of Communication.* Oxford: Berg.

Hughes-Freeland, F. 2007. 'Charisma and Celebrity in Indonesian Politics', *Anthropological Theory* 7(2): 177–200.

Hutchins, E. 1995. *Cognition in the Wild.* Cambridge, MA: MIT Press.

Infosoc Malaysia. 2002. URL (consulted June 2010): http://www.sabah.gov.my/infosoc/dailypress.asp.

Ingold, T. 2008. 'Bindings against Boundaries: Entanglements of Life in an Open World', *Environment and Planning* 40(8): 1796–1810.

Jayawardena, C. 1987. 'Analysis of a Social Situation in Acheh Besar: an Exploration of Micro-history', *Social Analysis*, Special Issue series, no. 22: 30–46.

Jean-Klein, I. 2003. 'Into Committees, Out of the House? Familiar Forms in the Organization of Palestinian Committee Activism during the First Intifada', *American Ethnologist* 30(4): 556–77.

Jenkins, R. 2002. *Pierre Bourdieu*, 2nd edn. London: Routledge.

Jensen, J.L. 2003. 'Public Spheres on the Internet: Anarchic or Government-Sponsored – A Comparison', *Scandinavian Political Studies* 26(4): 349–74.

John, K.J. 2002. 'Towards a K-Malaysia: Vision and Strategies. International Conference Partnership Networks as Tools to Enhance Information Society Development and Knowledge Economy', Moscow, 9 December 2002, URL (consulted June 2010): http://www.globalknowledge.ru/GKRussia/doc/John_en.ppt.

Johnson, K. 2001. *Television and the Social Change in Rural India.* New Delhi: Sage Publication.

Juris, J.S. 2008. *Networking Futures: the Movements against Corporate Globalization.* Durham, NC: Duke University Press.

Karim, M.R.A. and Khalid, N.M. 2003. *E-Government in Malaysia.* Subang Jaya: Pelanduk.

Kapferer, B. 2005. 'Situations, Crisis and the Anthropology of the Concrete: The Contribution of Max Gluckman', *Social Analysis* 49(3): 85–122.

Kavanaugh, A.L. and S.J. Patterson. 2002. 'The Impact of Community Computer Networks on Social Capital and Community Involvement in Blacksburg' in B. Wellman and C. Haythornthwaite (eds) *The Internet in Everyday Life*, 325–44. Oxford: Blackwell.

Keeble, L. and B.D. Loader (eds). 2001. *Community Informatics: Shaping Computer-Mediated Social Relations.* New York: Routledge.

Kelty, C. 2008. *Two Bits: The Cultural Significance of Free Software.* Durham, NC: Duke University Press.

———— 2009. 'This Is Not Your Mother's Samoa' (Review of Boellstorff's *Coming of Age in Second Life: An Anthropologist Explores the Virtually Human*), *Current Anthropology* 50(3), June 2009.

Klinenberg, E. 2005. 'Channeling into the Journalistic Field: Youth Activism and the Media Justice Movement' in R. Benson and E. Neveu (eds) *Pierre Bourdieu and the Journalistic Field*, 174–92. Cambridge: Polity Press.

Knappett, C. 2002. 'Photographs, Skeuomorphs and Marionettes: Some Thoughts on Mind, Agency and Object', *Journal of Material Culture* 7: 97–117.

Knox, H., M. Savage and P. Harvey. 2006. 'Social Networks and the Study of Relations: Networks as Method, Metaphor and Form'. *Economy and Society* 35(1): 113–40.

Krohn-Hansen, C. and K. Nustad (eds). 2005. *State Formation: Anthropological Perspectives*. Ann Arbor/London: Pluto.

Kubicek, H. and R.M. Wagner. 2002. 'Community Networks in a Generational Perspective: The Change of an Electronic Medium Within Three Decades', *Information, Communication & Society* 5(3): 291–319.

———, J. Millard and H. Westholm. 2003. 'The Long and Winding Road to One-stop Government'. Paper presented at an Oxford Internet Institute and Information, Communication, and Society Conference, Oxford, UK, 18 September 2003.

Landsman, Gail. 1987. 'Indian Activism and the Press: Coverage of the Conflict at Ganienkah'. *Anthropological Quarterly* 60(3): 101–13.

Leong, S.M.M. 2008. Social Imaginaries: a Working Model for Analysing the Internet's Wider Implications for the Internet. Unpublished Ph.D. thesis, Curtin University, Australia.

Loader, B.D. 2008. 'Social Movements and New Media'. *Sociology Compass* 2(6): 1920–33.

——— and L. Keeble. 2004. *Challenging the Digital Divide? A Literature Review of Community Informatics Initiatives*. York: Joseph Rowntree Foundation/YPS.

Loo, E. 2003. 'Opening Windows to "e-Democracy" in Malaysia'. Paper to the Hawaii International Conference on Arts and Humanities, URL (consulted March 2006): http://www.hichumanities.org/ AHproceedings/ Eric%20Loo.pdf.

Low, S. 2003. *Behind the Gates: Life, Security, and the Pursuit of Happiness in Fortress America*. New York and London: Routledge.

Lüders, M. 2008. 'Conceptualizing Personal Media', *New Media & Society* 10(5): 683–702.

Martin, J.L. 2003. 'What Is Field Theory?', *American Journal of Sociology* 109: 1–49.

Massey, D. 2005. *For Space*. London: Sage.

Mayer, A. 1966. 'The Significance of Quasi-Groups in the Study of Complex Societies' in Michael Banton (ed.) *The Social Anthropology of Complex Societies*, *ASA Monographs*, No. 4, 97–122. London: Tavistock.

McGee, T.G. and I.M. Robinson. 1995. *The Mega-Urban Regions of Southeast Asia*. Vancouver: UBC Press.

Melucci, A. 1996. *Challenging Codes: Collective Action in the Information Age*. Cambridge, UK: Cambridge University Press.

Meredith, D., L. Hopkins, S. Ewing and J. Thomas. 2002. 'Measuring Social Capital in a Networked Housing Estate', *First Monday* 7(10), URL (consulted March 2006): http://www.firstmonday.org/issues/issue7_10/meredyth/index.html.

Mesch, G.S. and Y. Levanon 2003. 'Community Networking and Locally Based Social Ties in Two Suburban Locations', *City and Community* 2: 335–52.

Miller, D. 2007. 'What is a Relationship? Is Kinship Negotiated Experience?' *Ethnos* 72(4): 535–54.

——— and D. Slater. 2000. *The Internet: An Ethnographic Approach*. Oxford: Berg.

Miller, L. 1995. 'Family Togetherness and the Suburban Ideal', *Sociological Forum*

10(3): 393–418.

Mitchell, J.C. (ed.). 1969. *Social Networks in Urban Situations.* Manchester: Manchester University Press.

Moeran, B. 2002. 'Fields, Networks and Frames: Advertising Social Organization in Japan'. *Global Networks* 16: 371–86.

——— 2005. *The Business of Ethnography: Strategic Exchanges, People and Organizations.* Oxford: Berg.

Moores, S. 2005. *Media/Theory.* London: Routledge.

Mulkay, M. 1985. *The Word and the World.* London: Allen and Unwin.

Nain, Z. 2004. 'New Technologies and the Future of the Media in Malaysia' in *Communicating the Future: Proceedings from the National Conference on the Future of Media in a Knowledge Society: Rights, Responsibilities and Risks.* Kuala Lumpur: UNDP and Strategic Analysis Malaysia (SAM).

Nair-Venugopal, S. 2001. *Language Choice and Communication in Malaysian Business.* Bangi: Penerbit UKM.

Newman, P. 1994. 'Opposing Development-led Planning – French-style', *Town and Country Planning.* July/August: 219–20.

Ng, A. 2002. SJ2005 Review. Unpublished PowerPoint presentation, MIMOS headquarters, Malaysia, 16 September 2002.

Nooy, W. de 2003. 'Fields and Networks: Correspondence Analysis and Social Network Analysis in the Framework of Field Theory', *Poetics* 31: 305–27.

Oldenburg, R. 1989. *The Great Good Place: Cafes, Coffee Shops, Community Centers, Beauty Parlors, General Stores, Bars, Hangouts, and How They Get You Through the Day.* New York: Paragon House.

Ooi, J. 2003. 'Local Governance: More Committees, More Meetings, More Studies'. Screenshots, 5 June 2003. URL (consulted June 2010): http://www.jeffooi.com

Pahl, R. 2005. 'Are all Communities Communities in the Mind?', *The Sociological Review* 53(4): 621–40.

Peterson, D.R. 2004. *Creative Writing: Translation, Bookkeeping, and the Work of Imagination in Colonial Kenya.* Portsmouth: Heinemann.

Peterson, M.A. 2003. *Anthropology and Mass Communication: Myth and Media in the New Millennium.* Oxford and New York: Berghahn Books.

——— 2010. '"But It Is My Habit to Read The Times": Metaculture and Practice in the Reading of Indian Newspapers' in B. Bräuchler and J. Postill (eds) *Theorising Media and Practice.* Oxford and New York: Berghahn Books.

Pigg, K.E. 2001. 'Applications of Community Informatics for Building Community and Enhancing Civic Society', *Information, Communication & Society* 4(4): 507–27.

——— and L.D. Crank. 2004. 'Building Community Social Capital: The Potential and Promise of Information and Communications Technologies', *Journal of Community Informatics* 1(1), URL (consulted March 2006): http://www.ci-journal.net/.

Pink, S. 2008 'Re-thinking Contemporary Activism: from Community to Emplaced Sociality'. *Ethnos* 73(2), 163–88.

―――― 2009. *Doing Sensory Ethnography.* London: Sage.

Pinkett, R. 2003. 'Community Technology and Community Building: Early Results from the Creating Community Connections Project', *The Information Society* 19: 365–79.

Postill, J. 2002. 'Clock and Calendar Time: A Missing Anthropological Problem', *Time and Society*, 251–70.

―――― 2006. *Media and Nation Building: How the Iban Became Malaysian.* Oxford and New York: Berghahn Books.

―――― 2007. Review of Evens and Handelman (eds) *The Manchester School: Practice and Ethnographic Praxis in Anthropology* (2006), Oxford: Berghahn, *Ethnos* 72: 4, 563–65.

―――― 2009. 'What is the Point of Media Anthropology?' *Social Anthropology* 17(3), 334–37, 340–42.

Putnam, D.R. 1995. 'Tuning In, Tuning Out: The Strange Disappearance of Social Capital in America', *Political Science and Politics* 28(4), 664–71.

―――― 2000. *Bowling Alone: The Collapse and Revival of American Community.* New York: Simon and Schuster.

Rafael, V. 2003. 'The Cell Phone and the Crowd: Messianic Politics in the Contemporary Philippines', *Public Culture* 15(3), 399–425.

Rapport, N. and V. Amit. 2002. 'Prologue: The Book's Questions' in V. Amit and N. Rapport *The Trouble with Community*, 1–12. London: Pluto.

Reis, F. 2006. 'Comunidades Radiofónicas: Um Estudo Etnográfico Sobre a Radiodifusão Local em Portugal'. Unpublished Ph.D. thesis, ISCTE, University of Lisbon.

Rheingold, H. 2002. *Smart Mobs: The Next Social Revolution.* Cambridge, MA: Perseus.

Riles, A. 2000. *The Network Inside Out.* University of Michigan Press.

Rogers, E.M. 1995. *Diffusion of Innovations*, 4th edn. New York: Free Press.

Roig, A. 2008. 'Cap al Cinema Col.laboratiu: Pràctiques Culturals i Formes de Producció Participatives'. Unpublished Ph.D. thesis, Universitat Oberta de Catalunya, Barcelona.

Saffo, P. 2007. 'Farewell Information, it's a Media Age', URL (consulted June 2010): http://www.saffo.com/essays/essay_farewellinfo.pdf.

Sanjek, R. 1996. 'Network Analysis', A. Barnard and J. Spencer (eds) *Encyclopedia of Social and Cultural Anthropology*, 396–97. London: Routledge.

Scherer, J.C. 1988. 'The Public Faces of Sarah Winnemucca'. *Cultural Anthropology* 3(2), 178–204.

Schuler, D. 1996. *New Community Networks: Wired for Change.* New York: ACM Press.

―――― 2000. 'New Communities and New Community Networks' in M. Gurstein (ed.) *Community Informatics: Enabling Communities with Information and Communication Technologies*, 174–89. Hershey, PA: Idea Group.

Schulz, D.E. 2006. 'Promises of (Im)mediate Salvation: Islam, Broadcast Media, and the Remaking of Religious Experience in Mali'. *American Ethnologist* 33(2), 210–29.

Shearman, C. 1999. *Local Connections: Making the Net Work for Neighbourhood Renewal.* London: Communities Online.

Silverstone, R. and E. Hirsch (eds.). 1994. *Consuming Technologies: Media and Information in Domestic Spaces.* London: Routledge.

Singh, B. 2009. 'Malaysia in 2008: The Elections that Broke the Tiger's Back', *Asian Survey* 49(1), 156–65.

Skinner, J. 2009. 'Cyber Ethnography and the Disembedded Electronic Evergreen of Montserrat', M. Srinivasan and R. Mathur (eds) *Ethnography and The Internet: An Exploration,* 125–48. Hyderabad: ICFAI University Press.

Smith, L.C. 2006. 'Mobilizing Indigenous Video: the Mexican Case'. *Journal of Latin American Geography* 5(1), 113–28.

Sparks, J.R. and J.A. Schenk. 2001. 'Explaining the Effects of Transformational Leadership: An Investigation of the Effects of Higher-order Motives in Multilevel Marketing Organizations', *Journal of Organizational Behavior* 22, 849–69.

Stillman, L. and R. Stoecker. 2005. 'Structuration, ICTs, and Community Work', *Journal of Community Informatics* 1(3), URL (consulted August 2007): http://ci-journal. net/index.php/ciej/article/view/216.

Strauss, P. 2007. 'Fibre Optics and Community in East London: Political Technologies on a "Wired-Up" Newham Housing Estate'. Unpublished Ph.D. thesis, Manchester University, UK.

Street, B. 2000. 'Literacy Events and Literacy Practices' M. Martin-Jones and K. Jones (eds) *Multilingual Literacies: Comparative Perspectives on Research and Practice,* 17–29. Amsterdam: John Benjamin.

Swartz, D. 1997. *Culture & Power: The Sociology of Pierre Bourdieu.* Chicago: University of Chicago Press.

———, V. Turner and A. Tuden (eds). 1966. *Political Anthropology.* Chicago: Aldine Publishing Co.

Taylor, W. 2004. *Community Informatics In Perspective.* Hershey, PA: Idea Group.

Theophilus, C. 2002. 'Red Tape, Unpublished Wrongs Breed Graft in Local Councils: Survey', *Malaysiakini,* 17 May 2002.

Thompson, J.B. 1995. *The Media and Modernity: A Social Theory of the Media.* Cambridge: Polity Press.

Thrift, N. 2006. *Space, Theory, Culture & Society* 23, 139–55.

Tsagarousianou, R. 1998. 'Electronic Democracy and the Public Sphere: Opportunities and Challenges' in R. Tsagarousianou, D. Tambini and C. Bryan (eds) *Cyberdemocracy: Technology, Cities and Civic Networks,* 167–78. London: Routledge.

Turner, T. 2002. 'Representation, Politics, and Cultural Imagination in Indigenous Video: General Points and Kayapo Examples', F. Ginsburg, L. Abu-Lughod and B. Larkin (eds) *Media Worlds: Anthropology on New Terrain.* Berkeley: University of California Press.

Turner, V.W. 1974. *Dramas, Fields and Metaphors: Symbolic Action in Human Society.* Ithaca, NY: Cornell University Press.

Uimonen, P. 2003. 'Mediated Management of Meaning: On-line Nation Building in Malaysia', *Global Networks* 3(3), 299–314.

Van de Port, M. 2006. 'Visualizing the Sacred: Video Technology, "Televisual" Style, and the Religious Imagination in Bahian Candomblé', *American Ethnologist* 33(3), 444–61.

Venkatesh, M. 2003 'The Community Network Lifecycle: A Framework for Research and Action', *The Information Society* 19: 339–47.

Victoria Government 2002a. 'Cabinet directs councils to set up e-govt services', 19 May 2002, URL (consulted June 2010): http://www.egov.vic.gov.au/International/AsiathePacific/Malaysia/malaysia.htm.

———— 2002b. 'My Say: Shaping an e-government', 30 July 2002, URL (consulted June 2010): http://www.egov.vic.gov.au/International/AsiathePacific/Malaysia/malaysia.htm.

Wagner-Pacifici, R.E. 1986. *The Moro Morality Play: Terrorism as Social Drama*. Chicago, IL: University of Chicago Press.

Warde, A. 2005. 'Consumption and Theories of Practice', *Journal of Consumer Culture* 5, 131–53.

Warner, W.L. 1959. *The Living and the Dead: A Study of the Symbolic Life of Americans*. New Haven: Yale.

Webster, F. 1995. *Theories of the Information Society*. London: Routledge.

Wellman, B. 2001. 'Physical Place and Cyber Place: The Rise of Networked Individualism', *International Journal of Urban and Regional Research* 25, 2 (June 2001): 227–52.

———— 2002. 'Little Boxes, Glocalization, and Networked Individualism' in M. Tanabe, P. van den Besselaar and T. Ishida (eds) *Digital Cities II: Computational and Sociological Approaches*, 10–25. Berlin: Springer.

———— and B. Leighton. 1979. 'Networks, Neighborhoods and Communities', *Urban Affairs Quarterly* 14: 363–90.

————, A. Quan-Hasse, J. Boase, W. Chen, K. Hampton, II de Diaz, et al. 2003. 'The Social Affordances of the Internet for Networked Individualism', *Journal of Computer-Mediated Communication* 8(3), URL (consulted August 2007): http://jcmc.indiana.edu/vol8/issue3/wellman.html,

Wenger, E. 1998. *Communities of Practice: Learning, Meaning, and Identity*. New York: Cambridge University Press.

Werbner, R. 1990. 'South-Central Africa: the Manchester School and After' in R. Fardon (ed.) *Localizing Strategies: Regional Traditions of Ethnographic Writing*, 152–81. Edinburgh: Scottish Academic Press.

Wesch, M. 2008. 'An Anthropological Introduction to YouTube'. Presentation to the Library of Congress, 23 June 2008. URL (consulted June 2010): http://www.youtube.com/watch?v=TPAO-lZ4_hU.

Wittel, A. 2001. 'Toward a Network Sociality', *Theory, Culture & Society* 18(6): 51–76.

Yeoh, P.C. 2005 'The Jawatankuasa Penduduk (JKP) covering Subang Jaya/USJ and Sunway', URL (consulted August 2007): http://nwatch.net.my/topicOpen.cfm?start=1&count=10&id=25960A05-1584-4BE5-875EF359762CD9D3&.

Yong, J.S.L. 2003. 'Malaysia: Advancing Public Administration into the Information Age' in J.S.L. Yong (ed.) *E-Government in Asia: Enabling Public Service Innovation in the 21st Century.* Singapore: Times.

Zald, M.N. and J.D. McCarthy. 1988. *The Dynamics of Social Movements: Resource Mobilization, Social Control and Tactics.* Winthrop, 1979; reprinted Lanham, MD: University Press of America.

Zurawski, N. 2000. *Virtuelle Ethnizität.* Frankfurt am Main: Peter Lang.

Index